FARMHOUSE FARE

*A New Economy Edition
of Country Recipes*

Collected by

THE FARMERS WEEKLY

LONDON
THE FARMERS WEEKLY, LTD.

1st *Impression*
January, 1940

INTRODUCTION

THIS new edition of *Farmhouse Fare*, like its predecessor, is made up entirely of recipes contributed and well-tried by countrywomen scattered over the length and breadth of the country.

The dishes you will find here have not been concocted by experts with all the resources of a modern kitchen. They have been cooked by succeeding generations of women in the farmhouses of the British Isles: upon modern cookers, upon open fires, upon old-fashioned ranges; with every variety of fuel, from peat and oil to electricity.

Until the first *Farmhouse Fare* appeared, no such cookery book had ever been made. Its success astonished even ourselves. It became very plain that a far wider public than we expected had appreciated these recipes, and the good sense and good cooking that had gone into them. We watched the first edition sell itself much as a small boy, confident and delighted, watches his kite sail high and higher into the air.

Successive reprintings still have not kept pace with the demand. We had to decide whether to print again, or issue a new edition altogether. Times, as they say, were changing. More and more of these excellent recipes were constantly reaching us at the *Farmers Weekly* from all over the country. We decided on the new edition.

Those of you who already possess the little yellow book, to which this is a companion volume, will know what to expect here. Many of the original recipes remain; many new ones have been added. But they all share the same characteristic: they are all the traditional product of the farmhouse kitchen.

This is an economy edition; but not the kind of economy that consists of the dull substitution of one ingredient for another, a business of scrimping and saving and makeshift. We have not even, as you will find, altered the recipes ; where butter was written, butter remains. You who cook can make those substitutes for yourselves, and this is a cookery book not only for war-time but for happier times, too. Here is, instead, the sturdy honest kind of economy by which resourceful countrywomen have always made the best possible use of the materials closest at hand.

Some of those materials, like game and poultry, the townswoman is inclined to look on as a luxury. But they are still easily come by in most country places, and there is one thing this last war has done for us—it has turned many a townswoman into a countrywoman.

One thing, however, we have done. In each section we have included one or two recipes in which economy is, for once in a way, thrown overboard. Even in difficult times we need our celebrations. We should like to feel that this new edition of *Farmhouse Fare* will serve your merry-makings as well as your everyday needs.

Now I hand over the introductory chapters to Mrs. Arthur Webb, whose work for the *Farmers Weekly* is, as her readers know, the mainspring of this spontaneous contribution to the recorded cookery of her own country-side. And she, and the publishers, and I, gratefully record here our appreciation of the generous interest with which the real authors of this book—the senders of the recipes themselves—have collaborated with us.

MARY DAY.

Fill Your Cupboard Shelves

by MRS. ARTHUR WEBB

IT is said that the plainest meal of stale bread and tired cheese can be made interesting by the addition of pickled onions, or a spoonful of chutney; and that the skimpiest rations of " left overs " of meat, game or fish, can be considered worth eating if served in company with a tasty sauce. Surely, then, it is simple common sense to make sure that chutney, pickle, sauce, are within reach. Anything that, in the homely phrase, makes the mouth water brings appetite to aid digestion; and transforms food that might otherwise become monotonous.

Well-filled shelves are a proud possession; and one great advantage about pickles and chutneys is that they can be made with such simple everyday things.

Cauliflower, cabbage (red and green), marrow, onions, shallots, beetroot, beans (French and runner), gherkins, carrots and cucumbers—all these, as far as vegetables are concerned, are excellent. While as for fruit—tomatoes (ripe and unripe), damsons, plums, rhubarb, elderberries, gooseberries, lemons, pears, blackberries, cherries and apples are also ready in their season to help; some for pickles, and some in chutney. And one of our most prized pickles is that made with walnuts gathered, green and juicy, in July.

Whatever vegetables you choose for pickling, they must be young and in perfect condition; and prepared as soon after gathering as possible. If they are supposed to be fresh—let them *be* fresh; not stale-looking, with half their flavour gone.

Years ago people thought that the clever housewife was she who used the best of her fruits for jams and jellies, and allowed the surplus only to be eaten as fresh fruit or cooked for pies and puddings. Now we've altered all that; now it is considered wiser to eat the finest fruit *uncooked*, and to make the most of the remainder either by cooking for immediate use, or in the form of some preserve to store.

This matter of jam and jelly making has also changed during the last few years. Instead of the long boring job of standing and stirring the boiling fruit and sugar, not knowing how long the process would take, we can now promise definite results in much less time than once was considered possible. With my own methods, for instance, I know that after the sugar is added, raspberry, loganberry or red currant jam should set with five minutes boiling; green gooseberry with ten minutes;

blackcurrant with fifteen minutes; and strawberry with one minute's boiling. You can see the wonderful saving in fuel, labour and patience, to say nothing of the improved flavour and colour of the preserve: and the shorter time sugar is in the cooking, the less of it you need. Long continued boiling of jams usually produces a darkening of the colour, a hardening of the fruit, a reduction in the quantity owing to evaporation and depreciation of flavour.

Then, while fruits are fresh and firm, ripe and in perfection, they can be bottled; and while certain principles have to be followed, no difficult process is necessary. It is necessary, of course, to understand principles of bottling—why fruit decays and how decay can be prevented.

Decay is caused in two ways:

(a) By ferment contained in the fruit itself.

(b) By moulds and yeasts present in the air.

Decay proceeds more rapidly in warm weather, when raspberries or other soft fruit may go mouldy or start to ferment in a single night. To prevent this spoilage the moulds, yeasts and ferments must be destroyed, and this can be accomplished by means of moderate heat. Very high temperatures, chemicals and preservatives are not required. To state the process briefly: the fruit is heated in a bottle until the germs are killed; then the bottle is sealed to prevent re-infection. This process of heating and sealing comprises Fruit Bottling.

No expensive apparatus is necessary; but the special bottles with glass tops and screw bands, or spring clips, have many advantages—they look well, hold a lot, are easily managed and keep the contents absolutely air-tight. These bottles, when packed, can be sterilized in proper sterilizers, or in large pots, or big saucepans. The appearance of the sealed-down fruit is as attractive as that of the fresh fruit; and according to the sugar supply, they can be packed and filled up with either plain cold water or a simple syrup. This form of sterilizing takes 1 hour and 40 minutes (as there must be a gradual rise of temperature to 165°, and then it must be kept at that temperature for 10 minutes).

Where sterilizers and special boilers are not to hand, fruit can still be preserved; because ordinary jam jars of the 2 lb. or 3 lb. size will come to the rescue, and any oven heated by coal, gas, oil or electricity will serve for the simple process known as Oven Bottling. When fruit and bottles are hot right through, the jars are taken out one at a time; and the fruit is covered with water or syrup *boiling* hot, then sealed securely.

6

Oven Bottling is cheaper, quicker and easier than by the sterilizer method; but its appearance is not so good as the fruit does not keep its shape so well.

So much for fruit bottling. But in many gardens there is often also a surplus of vegetables, young, fresh and tender. Many of these could be preserved by bottling for winter use.

While the preserving of fruit is quite a simple matter, vegetables require very much more care; for instance, very thorough washing is necessary before any other preparation is made. As they grow in or near the ground, they are, of course, sure to have a lot of grit, dust, dirt, etc., on them. Then when they are peeled or shelled, according to their variety, they must be " blanched "; that is, tied in muslin, plunged into a pan of boiling water and kept at boiling point from 1 to 5 minutes, according to their kind. From the boiling water they should be put into cold water, and remain in it until they are packed. Because vegetables have little or no acid in them, it is necessary to supply acid to preserve them; and this is put into the liquid with which they are covered in the bottles. This so-called " Acid Brine " is made in these proportions:

> 1 *quart boiling water*
> 1 *tablespoonful lemon juice, strained*
> 2 *level teaspoonfuls bar salt*

stirred well together, and cooled before covering the packed vegetables. When the vegetables are put into the bottles they must be packed very loosely; otherwise they cannot sterilize properly, for the heat will not reach the centre of the bottle.

Acid brine must cover the contents of the jar when they are packed.

In sterilizing vegetables, the bottles must go into a sterilizer sufficiently deep to hold water to come right up over the tops of all the bottles. The water starting from cold can be brought quickly to boiling point and afterwards *boiling must be maintained for at least 1 hour and 30 minutes*. Before starting vegetable bottling, the very fullest directions should be secured to make the trouble worth while.

CANNING

We all owe such a great measure of gratitude to this method of preserving foods that no excuse is needed for introducing the subject as one for consideration. Speaking as one who has been canning plums, pears, cherries, strawberries, raspberries, peaches (so far as fruits are concerned) for the last twenty years,

7

and peas, runner and French beans, carrots, etc. (among the vegetables), I am certain that home canning is a most satisfactory way of securing a supply of delicious foods of home production.

The apparatus to start with may be rather expensive, but the chief item, the canning machine, need not be kept for the use of one household; it could easily be shared by several in a district. It should, however, be in charge of some one with the fullest knowledge of canning: of how each type of fruit or vegetable should be prepared, and of the immense importance of carrying out the special instructions which make for complete safety of the contents of the cans. When skilfully done, the cans will store safely packed in boxes, that may be kept in any dry cool place free from risk of damp or change of temperature.

DRYING

Herbs, which play so large a part in the housewife's skill as a cook, must have their place in the cupboard; and as exposure to light often tends to bleach green things, it is well to encase bottles containing dried parsley, mint, thyme, sage and marjoram within a little brown paper; paper-lined tins may be found more convenient as containers. But keep your dried herbs handy; for they are the finest of company when making simple savouries, forcemeat, etc.

Let the freshly-gathered herbs be very thoroughly rinsed through two or three lots of cold water. Then shake them well before putting a layer on small drying trays, and placing them in cool oven (with door ajar to let moisture escape) or in hot airing cupboards. When dried sufficiently they can be rubbed through a sieve or colander and stored away in separate receptacles.

Scarlet runners, young and fresh, may be sliced, blanched for a moment or so in boiling water, cooled and spread to dry, and then packed away.

Non-keeping onions can be cut in thin slices and dried; and apple rings cut from apples peeled and cored, if threaded on to canes and put in a very moderate oven or over a kitchen range, will be as good as (perhaps better than) those which the housewife has been in the habit of buying. The cooling oven, when the cooking is done, costs no more; and it should be called upon to help fill those cupboard shelves and preserve some of the dozens of items from orchards and garden.

More details concerning some of these methods will be found in the unique collection of recipes in the pages of this book.

SOUPS

MULLIGATAWNY SOUP

1 rabbit.
3 pennyworth good gravy bones.
4 pints water.
6 onions.
1 carrot.

1 turnip.
A little salt.
{ 6 tablespoonfuls flour.
{ 1 tablespoonful curry powder.
{ ½ pint water.

PREPARE the rabbit, boil in water till quite tender, take all the meat off, and put in a basin by itself. Put the gravy bones in the water the rabbit was boiled in, and boil for two hours. Strain through a sieve. Put back in saucepan. Mix the flour and curry powder with the ½ pint of water, and add to stock. Let it boil 15 minutes. Add the rabbit, and it is ready for serving.

A glass of port wine is an improvement.

From E. C. Pratt, Bedfordshire.

COCKIE LEEKIE

An old hen.
2 tablespoonfuls vinegar.
½ cupful rice.
4 large leeks.

¼ lb. prunes.
A good tablespoonful chopped parsley.

CLEAN the hen, put in cold water with the vinegar, and let it stand overnight. Wash well, and put on to boil; afterwards allowing to simmer until fairly tender (about 2½ hours). Add the rice and leeks, cook until tender: add the prunes (previously stewed and stoned) without the syrup. Add the parsley. Take out the hen, but put a few pieces of the breast back into the soup. Skim the fat off, and serve.

The remainder of the meat may be removed from the bones, reheated, and sent to table covered with egg sauce; and it will serve as a separate dish.

From Mrs. H. Nelson, Pembrokeshire.

WHITE SOUP

THIS is a nourishing soup in the warmer weather. Get an old fowl and after preparing it, put it on to boil with 3 quarts water, to which have been added a few pieces of turnip, 2 carrots and 2 onions. Let all simmer gently for 3 hours or until the fowl is cooked. Next add 2 pints sweet milk to which 4 table-spoonfuls ground rice have been stirred in. Let all simmer again for 10 minutes ; then add a tablespoonful chopped parsley, and salt and pepper to taste.

From Mrs. Cromar, Tillychardoch, Tarland, Aberdeenshire.

SCOTCH BROTH

1 lb. neck of mutton.	1 quart water.
1 turnip.	1 grated carrot.
1 onion.	1 tablespoonful rice.
½ teaspoonful chopped parsley.	Potatoes.
Seasoning.	

WIPE the meat and cut into neat joints. Put in a pan with the water, and season to taste. Bring slowly to the boil, and skim. Cut the vegetables into small pieces, wash the rice and put all into the pan. Let it simmer for 2 hours. Add the chopped parsley to the broth and serve at once.

From Miss Sarah Lund, Lancashire.

SHEEP'S HEAD BROTH
and a Potted Meat recipe for use with the same sheep's head

SOAK a sheep's head over night in cold, salted water. Pour off the next morning, wash well and place the head in a good-sized pan. Cover the head with water and put on to boil. Simmer for 30 minutes, skimming all the time, then add a good handful of peas, and the same quantity of barley ; both having previously been steeped. Add 2 carrots, 1 small turnip and 2 onions, all cut up into dice ; then 1 firm white heart of cabbage cut up. Simmer for 1 hour, then throw in a suet ball for each person. Simmer for another hour, taking the scum off as it appears. Remove from the fire and take the sheep's head out on to a plate. Serve the soup with squares of bread. For the suet balls, mix 2 ozs. suet, 3 ozs. flour, a little salt and water. Roll into balls in a little flour. See that the soup is boiling when the balls are put in.

After the sheep's head has cooled, remove all the meat from

the bone and put it through the mincing machine. Add salt, pepper and a good scrape of nutmeg, and stir it together with three tablespoonfuls of the clear liquor it has been boiled in. Press into small jars and run melted butter over the top.

From Mrs. M. Scott, Middleton St. George, Darlington, Durham.

IMITATION HARE SOUP

1 lb. gravy beef.	1 oz. flour.
1 onion.	1 quart stock.
1 carrot.	4 peppercorns.
1 turnip.	2 teaspoonfuls Worcester sauce.
1 oz. dripping.	

MELT dripping and fry the onion. Cut the meat very small, and remove the fat. Brown the flour in the pan when the meat is taken out. Cut the vegetables very small. Add cold liquid, and put everything in saucepan. Bring to the boil, and simmer for 1½ hours. Make forcemeat balls as below, and toss them in flour. Strain the soup and cook the balls in it for ½ hour.

Forcemeat balls :

1 tablespoonful breadcrumbs.	A little grated nutmeg.
½ tablespoonful chopped suet.	A little grated lemon rind.
1 teaspoonful mixed herbs.	Salt and cayenne pepper.
	1 egg.

Put all in a basin and mix to a stiff paste with the beaten egg. Make 6 balls.

From Miss F. Hopkins, Carnarvonshire.

RICH HARE SOUP

A large hare.	1 large wine-glassful port wine.
¾ lb. ham or bacon.	3 quarts beef stock.
2 onions.	A little salt and cayenne.
2 blades mace.	½ lb. breadcrumbs.
A bunch of thyme, parsley and sweet marjoram.	

CUT the hare into pieces, and the ham or bacon into slices. Put into a stewpan with the beef stock, onions, bunch of herbs and mace. Stew all together for about 2½ hours. Take out the bacon and pound all the inferior parts of the hare with it in a mortar. Strain the soup back into the stewpan, add the pounded meat and the breadcrumbs and the port wine. Simmer for nearly ½ hour. Rub through a sieve, season with a little salt and cayenne. Make it very hot, but do not let it boil, and serve it up quickly.

From Mrs. Rose H. Dancer, Northamptonshire.

OAT SOUP WITH CREAM (OR MILK)

1 cupful rolled oats.
4 teacupfuls white stock.
3 cloves.
1 teaspoonful sugar.

2 sliced onions.
1 little bayleaf.
Seasoning.
1 teacupful scalded thin cream or milk.

PUT the ingredients in a saucepan and simmer for 1 hour. Strain through a cheese-cloth, put again into a saucepan, and add the sugar and cream (or milk). Pour into a tureen which contains a lump of butter, a little salt and cayenne, and serve.

From Miss J. Harle, Durham.

CHEESE SOUP

A little butter or margarine.
1 tablespoonful finely chopped onion.
½ pint hot water.

1 pint milk.
2 tablespoonfuls flour.
Seasoning.
2 tablespoonfuls finely grated cheese.

FRY the onion, without browning, in the butter or margarine. When soft add the hot water. When the fragments of the onion are fully cooked, add the milk to increase the measure to about a quart, and as soon as it boils stir in the flour mixed smooth with milk. Season to taste, stir, and simmer till it thickens. A moment or so before serving, mix in the cheese.

From Miss Agnes S. Robertson, Lanarkshire.

WHITE VEGETABLE SOUP

2 lbs. potatoes.
2 lbs. carrots.
2 lbs. onions.
2 lbs. turnips.
1 level tablespoonful margarine.
Salt and pepper.

1 rounded tablespoonful chopped parsley.
1 rounded teaspoonful sugar.
1 rounded teaspoonful fine sago.
6 breakfastcupfuls water.
1 breakfastcupful milk.

PREPARE the carrots, turnips, onions and potatoes, and cut them into fine dice. Melt the margarine, and sweat the vegetables in it for 20 minutes. Add the water, sugar and seasoning, and bring to boiling point. Remove any scum caused by vegetables. Simmer from 1 to 1½ hours until vegetables are tender. Then wash sago, mix with a little water, add, and allow to simmer till sago is clear, which will take 20 minutes. Add milk and reheat. Place the chopped parsley in a tureen, and add the soup.

From Mrs. G. Neaves, Kent.

SPRING SOUP

1 large lettuce.	1 tablespoonful cornflour.
12 spring onions.	Parsley.
1 pint milk.	Salt.
1 pint stock, or water.	Nutmeg.
Crusts of bread.	Sugar.

Watercress, endive or sorrel may be used either with, or in place of, the lettuce for a change.

WASH lettuce and onions, shred lettuce, and slice onions thinly. Melt dripping in saucepan, and fry lettuce and onions for about 5 minutes. Add stock and part of milk, and let simmer gently for 10 minutes. Mix cornflour with remainder of milk, pour into soup, and stir until it boils, allowing to simmer for another 10 minutes. Season to taste with pepper, salt, sugar and a little nutmeg. Cut crust of bread into thin strips, dry quite crisp in oven, put into tureen with parsley picked small, and pour soup over. *From Miss F. Hughes, Denbighshire.*

POTATO SOUP

1 lb. potatoes.	1 oz. margarine.
2 small onions.	1 pint water.
1 dessertspoonful sago.	Salt and pepper.

PEEL potatoes and onions, and cut in slices. Put them into a saucepan with the margarine, put on the lid and let them cook together for 5 minutes or so. Shake the pan from time to time. Add water and simmer gently for about an hour. Then add the milk and the sago, and cook until the sago is transparent. Season, and serve hot.

From Joyce Mustill, Cambridgeshire.

VEGETABLE MARROW SOUP

1 large onion.	2 pints white stock.
1 large marrow.	2 ozs. flour.
2 ozs. dripping.	Salt and pepper.
1 pint milk.	

MINCE the onion finely. Peel and cut up the marrow and remove seeds. Melt 1 oz. of the dripping in a pan, add the marrow and onion, and steam for 20 minutes. Add the milk and stock, and cook until marrow is tender. Then rub through a sieve, melt the second ounce of dripping, add it to the soup, together with the flour and seasoning ; and stir until it boils. *From Mrs. H. Cobley, Leicestershire.*

TOMATO SOUP

6 tablespoonfuls tinned tomatoes.
1 pint milk : 1 oz. butter.

Pepper and salt to taste.
1 teaspoonful sugar.
Pinch bi-carbonate of soda.

PUT the tomatoes into a saucepan with the bi-carbonate of soda ; when they present a frothy appearance, add butter, sugar, pepper and salt, boil the milk and pour it over the tomatoes and stir until it boils. The soup is now ready for use. If preferred it may be strained. Serve with a little paprika.

From Mrs. Burton, Kirby Gate Farm, Melton Mowbray.

GREEN SOUP

DON'T throw away pea pods. Wash them thoroughly in salt water. Put into a pan with water, salt, an onion, carrot and bunch of herbs. Boil until tender (on the back of the stove all the afternoon), then pass through a sieve. Thicken with a little cornflour and butter. *From Miss R. Overington, Surrey.*

PEA SOUP WITHOUT MEAT

1 pint dried whole peas.
3 quarts water.
3 medium-sized turnips.

4 onions : 4 carrots.
Oatmeal : Pepper and salt.

SOAK the peas all night ; next day put them into 3 quarts of boiling water, boiling them till tender. Take them out, smash them together so as to form a paste, put them back into the water with the turnips and carrots (cut into dice) and the sliced onions. Let the soup simmer gently for 2 hours, then thicken with oatmeal and season with pepper and salt.

From Mrs. S. A. Ladd, Pembrokeshire.

HARICOT BEAN SOUP

1 lb. haricot beans.
1 peeled turnip : 1 stick celery.
2 ozs. dripping.
Sprig parsley : 2 tomatoes.

2 Spanish onions.
2 quarts water : 1 pint milk.
Pinch ground mace.
Salt and pepper.

SOAK beans in cold water overnight. Next day drain and add to water with mace, diced vegetables, pepper and dripping. Bring to boil and simmer for 3 hours, adding the sliced tomatoes 30 minutes before the soup is ready. When ready, rub through a wire sieve and add milk, minced parsley, and salt to taste. Reheat and serve. For 6 or 8 people.

Mrs. J. R. Robinson, Long Sowerby, Carlisle.

FISH

STUFFED HERRINGS

WASH and dry four fresh herrings. Remove heads, split them open, and take out backbone. Cook the roes gently in boiling water and then chop them. Mix with them 1½ table-spoonfuls of breadcrumbs, 1 tablespoonful melted butter, 1 teaspoonful anchovy essence, ⅛ teaspoonful chopped onion; season with salt and pepper. Close them, brush over with warm butter, and bake in moderate oven for 20 minutes. Serve with mustard butter; which is made as follows: Mix 1 oz. of butter with 1 teaspoonful dried mustard and 1 teaspoonful lemon juice. When thoroughly mixed together form into little pats and put one on top of each herring.

From Miss G. Beck, Central Blissville, Sunbury Co., N.B.

SOUSED HERRINGS

4 or more herrings. Seasoning to taste.
1 onion. Vinegar.

WASH and scale the herrings, cut off the heads and take out the backbones. Slice the onion finely, season with salt and pepper, and lay in a pie-dish. Roll up fish tightly, and place over the onions. Cover with vinegar and a little water, and bake in a slow oven for about an hour.

From Mrs. A. Darnell, Derbyshire.

SCALLOPED ROES

PLACE ½ lb. of herring's roes in a saucepan; cover with water, to which a little salt and vinegar has been added; boil until firm. Then butter a pie-dish, put a layer of brown bread-crumbs and a layer of the cooked roes alternately in the dish, sprinkle with salt and pepper; finish with breadcrumbs, and add a few knobs of butter on the top. Bake in a moderate oven until brown and serve very hot.

From Mrs. M. G. Ann, Ilex Grove, Tenby, S. Wales.

KROMESKIES

(This is a very good way of using up herring roes)

6 croûtons of bread.   3 rashers of bacon.
6 soft roes.   2 tomatoes.

SKIN tomatoes, cut into slices, and bake on a greased baking
sheet in a moderate oven. Cut rashers in half, wash roes,
and roll each roe in a piece of bacon. Dip in the following
batter and fry. Fry croûtons of bread first, and keep tomatoes
and croûtons hot while frying roes.

Batter :
2 ozs. flour.   ½ gill tepid water.
1 white of egg.   1 dessertspoonful salad oil.

Mix flour into a smooth dough with water and salad oil.
Beat up white of egg stiffly and fold into batter.

Lay the cooked tomato slices on the fried croûtons, and the
roes on top of the tomatoes. Serve hot.

From Miss H. Butler, Hertfordshire.

STUFFED HADDOCK

CLEAN a medium-sized haddock, keeping it whole. Dry
it, and rub a little salt down the backbone. Make a stuffing
with 2 teacupfuls breadcrumbs, 2 teaspoonfuls chopped parsley,
1 oz. chopped suet, pepper and salt to taste, and a little milk
to bind : stuff the fish, and sew or tie up with tape, and lay in a
greased dish. Shake some flour over the fish, dot with butter
or dripping, and bake for 20 minutes. Serve, garnished with
slices of lemon and sprigs of parsley.

From Mrs. E. Symes, Brockmill, Beal, Northumberland.

HADDOCK PUFFS

½ lb. cooked haddock.   Salt and cayenne to taste.
Liquor in which haddock was   ½ oz. finely chopped parsley.
    boiled.   2 eggs.
2 ozs. self-raising flour.   Milk.

FLAKE the haddock with a little of the liquor it was boiled
in, add the flour, seasoning and eggs, and add sufficient milk
to make the mixture of a soft consistency like sponge sandwich
dough. Have ready some very hot fat, and drop in tablespoonfuls of the mixture. Fry until golden brown. They will puff
up beautifully.

Serve very hot, with mashed potatoes.

From D. G. Peard, Devonshire.

SALMON PIE

MASH the cooked fish well with a fork, and place a layer in a buttered pie-dish. Cover with mashed potatoes well seasoned with salt and pepper, and then with a layer of finely-shredded onions. Repeat until the dish is nearly full, covering with a thick layer of white sauce. Put the dish in a moderate oven, and bake for about an hour. This is almost equally good made with tinned salmon. *From Mrs. G. M. Harris, Shropshire.*

SALMON IN CUSTARD

1 small tin of salmon.   ½ pint milk.
2 eggs.   Seasoning.

FLAKE the salmon with a fork and season well. Place in a greased fireproof dish. Pour over a custard made with 2 eggs beaten in the milk, and bake in the oven for about 30 minutes till set. To prevent the custard boiling, stand the dish in a shallow tin with a little water in it. Serve either hot or cold. This quickly-prepared dish is excellent for the summer supper table. *Mrs. R. Duckett, Keinton-Mandeville, Taunton.*

FISH PIE

1½ lbs. fresh filleted haddock.   Chopped parsley.
½ lb. soaked bread-crusts.   Seasoning to taste.
1 large cupful grated suet.   1 egg.

WASH the haddock and put in a fireproof pie-dish. Make a forcemeat of the other ingredients, binding together with the egg. Cover the fish with forcemeat and bake in a hot oven.

This can be prepared beforehand, and a hot tea or supper served without any trouble. *From Mrs. W. Woodcock, Yorkshire.*

SAVOURY FISH CUTLETS

Cutlets of hake or cod.   Tomatoes.
Small lump of butter.   Flour.

WELL grease a baking-dish. Slice tomatoes and arrange them in a layer with fish cutlets on top. Add another layer of tomatoes, cover with water and small dabs of butter, and bake in a quick oven for 25 minutes. Strain stock and thicken with flour to make a sauce.

Serve with potatoes or thin slices of toast.

From Margaret Brooke, Worcestershire.

POULTRY AND GAME

FOWL PIE

1 old fowl.
2 chopped onions.
1 stick of celery.
½ lb. ham, cut small.

A blade of mace, a few peppercorns, a little thyme, tied in a
muslin bag.
3 hard-boiled eggs.
Some chopped parsley.

PREPARE the fowl and cut into neat pieces, and put into a
saucepan with the onions, celery, and ham and seasoning
bag ; salt, of course, should be added. Cover with cold water,
bring to the boil and simmer till quite tender. Turn out and
leave till cold ; then remove the fat, and seasoning bag. Have
ready 3 hard-boiled eggs and some chopped parsley. Put a layer
of fowl in a pie-dish, with some of the gravy, and a layer of eggs
and parsley alternately with the meat until the dish is filled.
Cover with a good pastry crust and bake in a brisk oven till the
pastry is nicely browned.   *From Miss C. Ball, Bedfordshire.*

TWO DISHES FROM ONE FOWL

PREPARE chicken or boiling fowl, removing both legs.
Boil the giblets, 1 small onion, 2 or 3 slices of carrot, a little
celery in water to cover for 1 hour, adding a few peppercorns
and salt to taste. Strain and replace in the pan. Put in the
trussed chicken ; add sufficient water or stock just to cover the
chicken. Simmer gently till tender ; when cool, cut into pieces,
removing any protruding bone.

Meanwhile, boil the stock, with any trimmings, for 1 hour
or till reduced to 1 pint. Pour in a dish to make a layer of 1 in.
Melt 2 oz. of butter, blend in 2 oz. of flour, stir in 1 pint of
milk ; cook, stirring over gentle heat till thick. Coat each piece
of chicken separately ; place the pieces on the layer of jelly.
Decorate with cooked pieces of turnip and carrot, cut in pretty
shapes, add slices of tomato and cucumber. Serve cold.

STUFFED Legs of Fowl.—Remove the bone without breaking
the skin. For each leg allow ¼ lb. of sausage meat or veal

passed through a mincer. Season to taste, add any flavouring liked; with sausage meat, a little chopped ham or tongue. Or add to the veal a few breadcrumbs. Press the forcemeat inside the legs, form them into plump rolls, tie in muslin, simmer gently with the fowl for 1 hour or till tender. Serve cut in thick slices with a good brown gravy.

From Miss E. Fulton, Harehope, Eglingham, Northumberland.

CHICKEN IN BATTER

1 chicken.	1 teacupful flour.
2 eggs.	Cupful cold water.
1 tablespoonful salad oil.	1 onion.
A little gravy.	3 sprigs of parsley.
2 tomatoes.	Salt.

PARBOIL the chicken, sprinkle with salt, and let it cool a little. Beat the yolks of 2 eggs with a pinch of salt. Stir in the salad oil and the gravy. Mix in the flour, then pour in the water. Stand this one side to set. Take the onion, parsley, tomatoes, chop them finely and stir into the batter. Add the whipped whites of 2 eggs. Cut the chicken into neat pieces. Dredge with flour. Dip in batter and fry. Serve with rolls of fried bacon.

From Miss A. E. Parry, Flintshire.

A TASTY HOT-POT

A boiling fowl.	3 sprays each of parsley and thyme.
Flour.	Water or stock, seasoned.
2 onions.	A few fresh cooked green peas, or
2 carrots : 1 small parsnip.	a tin of peas.

SEPARATE all the joints of the fowl, as you would a rabbit. Flour well and put in a stew-jar with onions, carrots and parsnip (sliced up), and the parsley and thyme, tied in muslin. Cover with water or stock, seasoned. Cook gently for about 2½ hours. Thicken with a little flour and water, if necessary, about ½ hour before it is done. For the last ¼ hour, add the peas.

From Mrs. C. H. Davenhill, Staffordshire.

TO COOK AN OLD DUCK

DUCKS up to the age of 5 years may be cooked in this way : Truss and stuff as for roasting. Melt ¼ lb. of dripping in a saucepan. When hot, put in the duck and braise for about 15 minutes, turning twice. Add a breakfastcupful of cold water, cover closely and simmer for 4 hours.

From Mrs. Montgomery, Winford Manor, near Bristol.

BOILED DUCK

WHEN table ducks are plentiful, here is a recipe for boiling them.

Take a nice plump duck, and salt it for 24 hours by placing it in an earthenware vessel, and sprinkling a handful of salt over it. Take it out next day, wash it, and let it stand in cold water for about $\frac{1}{2}$ hour. Tie it in a cloth and put into a saucepan of boiling water; to which add 2 tablespoonsful of chopped sage and mint, and 3 medium-sized onions. Boil slowly until tender, about 2 hours. Serve with onion sauce and green peas.

From Mrs. O. Done, Chipnal Lees Farm, Cheswardine.

PARTRIDGE EN CASSEROLE

Brace of birds.
4 onions.
2 rashers of bacon.
2 carrots.
2 ozs. diced bacon.

Pepper and salt.
Sprinkling of chopped parsley and thyme.
1 savoy cabbage.
Stock made from " trimmings."

TRUSS the birds and place an onion inside each one and a rasher of bacon over each. Put them in a casserole with sliced carrots and onions cut into rings, the diced bacon, pepper and salt, and the parsley and thyme. Parboil the cabbage, drain it and cut into four. Pack this round the birds in the casserole, cover with boiling stock, and simmer gently for 3 hours. Serve in the casserole. *From Mrs. K. Porter, Leicestershire.*

OLD NORFOLK PARTRIDGE STEW

Brace of partridges.
Oil, lard, butter or dripping.
1 or 2 slices lean ham.
Clove of garlic.
1 tomato.

6 small mushrooms.
4 cloves.
6 peppercorns.
Salt water or stock.

CUT up the birds into joints or halves, fry in a little oil or dripping, then put them into a stew-pan with the slices of ham, clove of garlic, tomato, mushrooms, cloves, peppercorns, salt and enough water or stock to cover them. A glass of port may be added if you wish. Simmer the birds very slowly for 2 hours; when they will be tender enough to melt in the mouth, yet not in the least stringy or overdone. Serve them on a dish, heaped up, surrounded by the gravy; which has been freed from fat, thickened and made very hot. Garnish the dish with triangles of toast.

From Mrs. W. Gibbons, Norfolk.

TURKEY LOAF

CAREFULLY remove the bones from the remains of the turkey, and pass the flesh through a fine mincer, with a little onion. Season well with salt, pepper, and a little gravy and beaten egg. Roll tightly in a cloth, and boil for 1½ hours in boiling water, to which an onion and carrot have been added. Remove the cloth and serve hot. If wanted cold, glaze later.

From Miss Jerrams, Church Farm, Lillingstone Lovell, Buckingham.

WOOD-PIGEONS

2 wood-pigeons.
Seasoned flour.
2 slices of fat raw bacon.
2 large Spanish onions (or their equivalent bulk in home-grown ones).
About 6 large leaves of sage.
Good beef dripping or lard.
Hot water.
Seasoning.
1 meat cube.
Cornflour.

PICK and clean the wood-pigeons, cut them through lengthwise and cover with seasoned flour. Cut the bacon in dice and fry to extract the fat. Place the bacon in a stewpan, leaving the fat in the frying pan, into which put the onions and sage leaves. Fry together till onions are tender ; then add them to the bacon already in stewpan, still leaving the liquor in frying pan and adding to it the dripping or lard in which to fry the birds till browned all over. Lay the pigeons on the onions and pour over them all the liquor from the frying pan. Add hot water just to cover the bed of onions : cover closely, and allow to simmer till the birds are tender—about 1½ hours. When nearly done, season and add the meat cube. If necessary add a little more hot water, then thicken with cornflour. Serve with onion sauce and green peas. *From Mrs. Sara. Wilson, Hampshire.*

POTTED PIGEON

3 pigeons.
Pepper and salt.
A dash of Worcester sauce, if liked.
A little melted butter.

SKIN and clean the pigeons. Place them in a pan, cover with water and boil until the meat is leaving the bones. Remove from fire and, when cool enough to handle, carefully take away all bones and mince meat finely. Put the bones back into the saucepan and boil until the water has reduced to about 1 cupful. Season and add the Worcester sauce, if liked. Moisten the mince with stock from bones and a little melted butter. Press into jars and run a little melted butter on the top to seal each jar.

From Mrs. Stanley White, Cheshire.

JUGGED PIGEONS

4 pigeons.
2 hard-boiled eggs.
1 raw egg.
A sprig of parsley.
1 lemon.
A little suet.
A little flour.
Breadcrumbs.
Pepper and salt.

Nutmeg.
A little fresh butter.
1 head of celery, or a little celery salt.
A bunch of sweet herbs.
4 cloves.
A little mace.
A glass of white wine.

PICK and draw the pigeons, wiping very dry. Boil the livers a minute or two, and mince fine. Bruise with a spoon and mix with the yolks of the hard-boiled eggs, a sprig of parsley, chopped lemon peel, suet, breadcrumbs, pepper, salt and nutmeg. Mix in the raw egg and the butter. Stuff pigeons (including crops), dip them into warm water, dredge with pepper and salt, and put them into a jar with the celery or celery salt, sweet herbs, cloves, mace and white wine. Cover jar closely, and set it in a pan of boiling water for 3 hours. When pigeons are done, strain gravy into a stew-pan, stir in a knob of butter rolled in flour, cook until thick, then pour over pigeons. Garnish with slices of lemon. *From Mrs. George Marchant, Somersetshire.*

SOMERSET ROOK PIE WITH FIGGY PASTRY

6 rooks.
Weak stock.

Pieces of fat bacon cut in chunks.
Pepper and salt to taste.

For the paste :

1 lb. flour.
½ lb. fat.
4 ozs. currants.

4 ozs. raisins stoned.
Pepper and salt to taste.

BAKE the rooks, which must have been skinned ; using only the legs and breast, as all other parts are bitter. They should be left soaking in salt and water over night. In the morning drain away the brine and put the legs and breast in a good-sized pie-dish, adding the fat bacon. Cover with the stock, and season well with the pepper and salt.

For the Paste : Rub the fat well into the flour, adding pepper and salt, then add the currants and raisins. Mix well, and add sufficient water to make a stiff paste. Roll out to about ¾ in. thick, then place right over the pie, letting it come well over the sides. Cover the pie with a piece of greaseproof paper, and then put the pudding cloth on top. Tie well down and see that the water has no chance of getting in. There must be sufficient water in your boiler to cover it. Do not put the pie in until the water is boiling. The pie takes a good 3 hours to cook, and is delicious served with goosberry jelly.

From Miss G. M. Dinham, Wiltshire.

SUFFOLK JUGGED HARE

1 hare.
A bunch of sweet herbs.
2 onions (each stuck with 3 cloves).
6 whole allspice.
½ teaspoonful black pepper.

A strip of lemon peel.
Thickening of butter and flour.
2 tablespoonfuls ketchup.
Little port wine if liked.

WASH hare and cut into small joints, flouring each piece. Put these into a stew-pan with herbs, onions, cloves, allspice, pepper and lemon peel. Cover with hot water, and let it simmer until tender. Take out pieces of hare, thicken the gravy with the butter and flour and add ketchup and port wine. Let this boil for 10 minutes, then strain through a sieve over the hare and serve very hot.

Do not omit to serve red currant jelly with it. It is seasonable from September to the end of February. Rabbit cooked in a similar fashion is equally tasty. *From Miss O. M. Fincham, Suffolk.*

HARVEST RABBIT

Allow 1 small rabbit to every two persons.
Dripping.
3 prunes to each rabbit.
A bunch of fresh herbs to each rabbit.

Seasoned flour.
Onions (large, or salad onions).
1 thin slice of fat bacon to each rabbit.
Stock.

Forcemeat balls :

Chopped bacon (or suet).
Chives (or young onion tops).
Sweet marjoram.
Parsley.

Seasoning.
Breadcrumbs.
1 or 2 eggs.

SKIN, draw and cut off the heads, scuts and feet of the rabbits. Wash well, leave in salt water for 15 minutes, then dry and fry whole in dripping until a pale golden brown all over. Drain, and stuff under the ribs of each 3 well-soaked prunes and a bunch of fresh herbs. Coat thickly with well-seasoned flour. Cover the bottom of a large deep baking dish with thinly sliced onions, or the bulbs of salad onions, lay the floured rabbits on them, with a thin slice of fat bacon over each, and just cover with stock. Bake slowly for 2 hours. Serve on a hot dish, garnished with the onions and plenty of large forcemeat balls, made of the ingredients above bound with the egg, or 2 eggs if as many as 3 rabbits are cooked. Fry a deep brown, and be sure that plenty of fresh herb is used, as they must cut a bright green. Strain the gravy, and serve separately.

From Mrs. Jennifer Dane, Buckinghamshire.

RABBIT PUDDING WITH MUSHROOMS

2 young rabbits cut up in joints.
A few slices of fat bacon.
4 large sage leaves chopped fine.
Tablespoonful chopped onion.

Pepper and salt to taste.
¼ lb. suet.
½ lb. flour.
Good plate of mushrooms.

LINE a good-sized pudding basin with a suet crust, put in a layer of rabbit, chopped sage and onion, then a layer of peeled mushrooms, and continue until the basin is filled. Sprinkle plenty of flour between each layer, as that makes good thick gravy. The slices of bacon should be cut up in thin strips and put in each layer. Nearly fill the basin with water, cover with suet crust, and steam for about 3 hours. This is a very tasty and nourishing dish.

From Mrs. E. Arthur Hurst, Buckinghamshire.

GIPSY PIE

1 tender rabbit.
½ lb. beef steak.
2 teaspoonfuls chopped parsley.

¼ lb. cooked ham or pork sausages.
Salt, pepper and nutmeg.
Stock.

SOAK rabbit in cold salted water for 1½ hours. Wipe dry, joint; slice ham; or skin sausages, and with floured hands make meat into round balls. Cut steak in small pieces. Arrange rabbit, ham or balls, and beef in pie-dish. Sprinkle over the parsley grated nutmeg, pepper, salt to taste. Add stock, cover with pastry, and bake slowly for 1½ hours after the pastry has risen.

From Mrs. M. Stokes, Pant-Gwyn, Nebo, Penygroes, Caernarvon.

CURRIED RABBIT

1 rabbit.
½ lb. cooked rice.
1 lb. onions.
1 teaspoonful of curry powder.

2 ozs. butter.
A little flour.
Juice of ½ a lemon.

CUT the rabbit into joints, dust with flour, and fry each in fat until a nice brown. Cut up the onions and fry these, then dust in the curry powder and the rest of the flour. Put the rabbit into a saucepan, and cover with stock or water. Boil up, then add the onions, etc., and simmer for 1½ hours, or till the meat seems quite done. Heat the rice, squeeze the lemon juice over the rabbit, then pile the rabbit and curry in the centre of the dish with a wall of boiled rice around. Serve hot.

From Mrs. A. M. Helliar, Seymour Farm, Curland, Taunton.

OLD DEVONSHIRE RABBIT BRAWN

1 large rabbit.	Pepper.
2 pig's trotters.	Spice.
Salt.	Water.

PUT 2 pig's feet in a saucepan with cold water to cover and boil gently for 1½ hours. Then put in with them a rabbit which has been prepared and soaked in salted water for ½ hour to whiten the flesh. Boil all together for 2 hours, or until the flesh is tender and leaves the bones easily ; adding more water in the meantime if needed. Remove from the fire, and when cool enough, take out all the bones, cut the meat in small pieces, and season with salt, pepper and spice to suit taste. Boil all up together, then put into 2 moulds or pudding basins previously rinsed with cold water. Let it stand overnight, turn out, and serve with a dish of lettuce and tomatoes.

This make s a very good meat course for luncheon or supper, and is fit to put before any one—as the saying is.

From Mrs. B. Heal, Devonshire.

HAM AND CHICKEN BRAWN

1 chicken.	Pepper and salt.
1 lb. ham or streaky bacon.	Bunch of herbs tied in muslin.
	Nutmeg, or flavour to choice.

AT the time of the year when farmers have last year's stock cockerels to dispose of, a good way of using them will be welcomed. Here is one.

Kill the bird and put in a small bath or bowl. Pour boiling water over it to get the feathers off. This is much easier than plucking, and cleans the skin. Then remove inside and cut up the joints, and simmer 3 hours in just enough water to cover. Put in any flavouring cared for, such as nutmeg, pepper and salt, and herbs. Cook the ham or bacon with the bird. When cooked cut up in very small pieces. Swill out a large cake tin with water and pack the pieces in it ; and then strain enough of the gravy over to make it jelly between. This makes a good brawn. It does not need any pressing and sets nicely.

From Mrs. A. Disney, Devonshire.

CHICKEN GALANTINE

1 fairly large fowl.
1 egg.
1 lb. sausage meat.
6 ozs. ham or tongue.
1½ pints white stock.
2 hard-boiled eggs.
Pepper and salt.

1 teaspoonful chopped parsley.
Glaze.
Aspic jelly.
Grated rind of ½ a lemon.
2 ozs. breadcrumbs.
A pinch of herbs.

BONE the fowl. Make a stuffing with the sausage meat, breadcrumbs, seasonings and beaten egg. Cut the ham into square pieces. Place this inside the fowl, with the hard-boiled eggs cut in quarters. Sew up with fine string, and roll in a clean cloth. Bring the stock to boiling point, put in the fowl, and simmer gently for 2 to 2½ hours. When cold remove the cloth, glaze all over and dish up on a border of lettuce and cress, and garnish with chopped aspic jelly.

From Miss M. Ramage, Cheshire.

CHICKEN AND PORK BRAWN

1 old fowl.
2 pig's feet and hocks.

Seasoning.

SKIN and clean fowl and cut up into joints. Clean feet and hocks. Put all in saucepan and cover with cold water, bringing to boil and simmering gently for 4 hours. Strain and remove bones, cut up meat finely and season highly with pepper and salt. Boil again for 10 minutes. Press into a mould and allow to set.

From Miss C. Provan, Middlesex.

RABBIT PASTE

1 rabbit.
Lump of margarine size of egg.
1 lump sugar.
12 allspice.

6 peppercorns.
3 blades mace.
1 onion stuck with 12 cloves.

CUT rabbit into small joints, and put into casserole or jar with margarine and other ingredients. Cover closely and cook slowly until the meat will leave the bones easily. When cold put the meat through a mincer 2 or 3 times, then beat together with ½ lb. margarine, 1 dessertspoonful Worcester sauce and a little cayenne pepper and a teaspoonful more sugar. Put into small pots, and pour over a little melted butter or margarine.

From Mrs. M. R. Slade, Hampshire.

MEAT DISHES

TIPPERARY IRISH STEW PIE

½ lb. lean shin of beef.
3 carrots.
3 turnips.
1 onion.
1 pint of water.

Gravy browning.
6 large potatoes.
A few pieces of celery.
1 dessertspoonful seasoning.

Suet crust paste composed of :

¼ lb. flour.
2 ozs. suet.
¼ teaspoonful salt.

¼ teaspoonful baking powder.
½ gill water.

CUT up the meat into pieces 1 in. square. Put the meat into a casserole (one with a lid), and slice into this the onion, carrots, turnips, celery and seasoning. Add the water and simmer for an hour. Add the sliced potatoes and boil a further ¼ of an hour. Make the paste and roll it out, so that it will just fit into the casserole, and place on top of the stew. Put the casserole lid on : boil gently for ½ an hour.

From Mrs. G. Dean, Cheshire.

JUGGED STEAK

A thick piece of steak.
Cloves.
Celery.

2 onions.
1 teaspoonful mushroom ketchup.
Pepper and salt.

CUT the steak into pieces about 1 in. square, and put into a stone jar. Add the onions stuck with cloves, the celery, mushroom ketchup, pepper and salt. Cover the jar closely and place in a pan of boiling water. Let it simmer until the meat is tender : or it can be placed in the oven and left to stew for a couple of hours. Add no water or grease. When done it is like jugged hare.

From Mrs. P. Horsell, Berkshire.

BRAISED SHEEP'S TONGUES

3 sheep's tongues.   A few slices of bacon.
2 small turnips.   1 onion.
1 carrot.   A bouquet of herbs.

LAY the sheep's tongues in salt and water for 12 hours and then put them in cold water. Bring rapidly to the boil. Drain the tongues dry, fry a few slices of bacon in a stew-pan and in this put a sliced carrot, an onion and the turnips, with a bouquet of herbs. On this place the tongues, and lay another slice of bacon over them. Pour in a pint of stock and simmer gently for 3 hours. Skin the tongues, slice them lengthwise, and put the pieces in the stew-pan with the strained gravy till they are hot.   *From Miss A. E. Parry, Flintshire.*

SAVOURY SHEEP'S HEAD

1 sheep's head.   1 medium-sized onion.
½ lb. rice.   ¼ teaspoonful mixed herbs.
¼ lb. breadcrumbs.   Pepper and salt.

SOAK the head overnight in plenty of salt and water. Wash off well and boil very slowly for about 1½ to 2 hours with the onion. Add rice ½ hour before it is ready. When nearly cold, carefully cut the meat off the bones and mince or cut up very fine. Now mix the herbs, salt and pepper with the breadcrumbs. Well grease the pie-dish and put alternate layers of breadcrumbs, meat and rice ; top your dish with breadcrumbs. You may also add a skinned tomato, cut up, to decorate and give colour to your dish. Pour over a little gravy and brown in the oven for ½ hour. This dish can be prepared overnight and heated up in the morning, and is both nourishing and cheap.

     From Mrs. Stone, Glebe Farm, Kenn, Exeter, Devon.

MOCK GOOSE

1 bullock's heart.   8 or 10 large sage leaves, chopped
2 bay leaves.   fine.
4 cloves.   ¼ lb. chopped suet or bacon.
2 meat cubes.   ½ lb. breadcrumbs.
4 large onions, grated.   1 egg.
1 tablespoonful cornflour. Pepper and salt.
           Dripping.

WELL wash the heart and place in a saucepan with enough water to cover. Add the pepper and salt, bay leaves, cloves and meat cubes. Simmer gently for 4 or 5 hours on the side of the stove. (It must only simmer to ensure tenderness.)

Set aside until next day. Take off the fat from the stock. Mix together, with the egg to bind, the onions, sage leaves, chopped suet or bacon and breadcrumbs. Make into forcemeat balls, leaving a little to stuff the heart. Put the heart with the force-meat balls round it in a baking-tin, cover with dripping and bake in a sharp oven for ½ hour. Strain the stock in which the heart was boiled: use about 1 pint to thicken with the cornflour. This makes a good brown gravy to serve with the heart.

The remainder of the stock makes an excellent soup if all kinds of vegetables are cut up and added. Thicken with corn-flour. The remainder of the heart can be minced for next day's dinner, and served with brown gravy and baked potatoes.   *From Mrs. Arthur Hurst, Buckinghamshire.*

HEART AND KIDNEY PUDDING

For the crust :

½ lb. self-raising flour.	Salt.
¼ lb. shredded suet.	Cold water.

For the filling :

1 pig's heart.	1 tablespoonful flour.
2 pig's kidneys.	Salt and pepper.
	Water.

MIX together flour, suet and salt, and make into a soft dough with cold water. Roll out, and line a basin with part of the dough ; leaving enough over for a lid. Cut heart and kidneys into small pieces, after removing all deaf ears and skin ; roll in seasoned flour and add enough water to cover. Roll out remainder of the dough to make the lid. Cover with grease-proof paper and steam for 3 hours.

From Miss M. R. Whittall, Pentiken, Newcastle, Craven Arms, Salop.

HARICOT OX TAIL

1 ox tail.	½ lb. turnips.
½ lb. onions.	Salt and pepper.
1 dessertspoonful flour.	3 cloves.
1 oz. butter.	6 peppercorns.
½ lb. carrots.	1 teaspoonful chopped parsley.

JOINT ox tail and cut in pieces. Stick one onion with cloves and put in pan with parsley, peppercorns, seasoning, meat and enough water to cover. Bring to boil and simmer gently for 1 hour. Strain off gravy, and skim off the fat. Put gravy in the pan again with meat, and remainder of onions, peeled and sliced ; cut up carrots and turnips small. Simmer until vegetables are tender. Mix butter and flour and stir into the stew. Simmer for 10 minutes. Turn on to a hot dish and give a border of boiled haricot beans.

From Mrs. J. R. Robinson, Long Sowerby, Carlisle, Cumberland.

LAMB TAIL PIE

ON some farms it is the custom to cut off lambs' tails when the lambs are very young ; the tails then are small and not of much use. When left to get to a fair size, they make a delicious pie. When the tails are severed instruct the shepherd to keep them warm by covering with a sack.

Cut off the longest of the wool with scissors. Prepare the scald by putting 1 part cold to 3 parts of boiling water, and immerse the tails for a few minutes : then the wool will come off easily. Stew the tails in water with a carrot and onion, or in veal stock ; they will want to stew for some time if they are fairly big—some farmers' wives roll each tail in chopped parsley before putting into the pie-dish. Hard-boiled eggs may—or may not—be added. Cover with short crust, and bake. Brush with beaten egg when partly baked.

From Miss V. Grey, The Manor Farm, Banbury, Oxon.

FRICO

THIS is a very excellent and savoury dish. Take 2 lbs. of lean beef, fillet or any other juicy part, 2 lbs. of potatoes, and 1 lb. of Spanish onions, seasoning, butter, stock and claret as below. Cut the meat into thick pieces of 2 in. square, parboil the potatoes and slice thickly ; slice the onions and fry a yellow colour in butter for 10 minutes or so ; then put all into a jar, with onions top and bottom, together with the butter they were cooked in ; add pepper but no salt, add a pint of stock and a glass of claret. Tie down with greased paper, and cover the jar with the lid.

Cook in a gentle oven, setting the jar in a pan with the hot water half the depth of the jar, the contents of which must not reach boiling point. In 2 to 3 hours the meat will be tender ; then add salt to taste (nothing else, unless more pepper is needed) and serve in a hot, deep dish. If the meat is cooked slowly enough, there will be plenty of gravy.

From Mrs. F. Walker, The Grange Farm, Clavering, near Newport, Essex.

JARRETT STEAK

1½ lbs. "ordinary" steak.
A few sticks of celery.
6 small rolls of bacon.

1 cupful water.
1 tablespoonful Worcester sauce.
2 tablespoonfuls tomato sauce.
A little flour.

CUT the steak up into pieces 1 in. square, rolling each piece in flour, put in a casserole dish and add the celery, finely cut, and the bacon. Over this pour the water into which has been mixed the Worcester and tomato sauce. The meat should now be covered. Put in oven, boil up, and then allow to simmer 2 hours. Turn meat occasionally, and if too dry add a little water. If very mild bacon has been used, add a little salt.

From Mrs. T. H. Robinson, Gloucestershire.

BRISKET OF BEEF—PICKLED

6 lbs. salted brisket of beef.
3 slices of bacon.
2 carrots.
1 onion.

Bunch of savoury herbs.
Salt, pepper, cloves.
Allspice, mace.

PUT the beef in a stew-jar, together with the rest of the ingredients, and cover all with water. Stew gently in oven for 4 hours. When cooked leave to cool, then remove from the liquid and press between two plates under a weight.

From Alice Kilding, Yorkshire.

ROLLED STEAK AND PUFFS

SELECT 2 lbs. juicy steak, cut in one piece about ¾ in. thick. Make a seasoning as follows : Rub 1 teaspoonful dripping into 1 cupful fine breadcrumbs ; add a little mixed herbs, pepper and salt, and a small onion finely minced. Spread this mixture over the steak, roll up and fasten with a skewer. Dust over the roll a little flour and a pinch of sugar (the sugar imparts a delicious flavour and makes a nice brown gravy), place in a greased baking-dish, and put dripping on top. Roast about 1½ hours. Baste frequently.

About 20 minutes before it is cooked, pour into the dish, 1 dessertspoonful at a time, a Yorkshire pudding batter. For batter, beat 1 egg thoroughly, add ½ pint milk, sift in ¼ lb. flour and pinch of salt. Leave a space between the spoonfuls. When cooked, place roast on dish with Yorkshire puffs, and serve with brown gravy and vegetables.

From Mrs. H. Mewton, Callestick, Truro, Cornwall.

SWISS STEAK

TAKE 2 lbs. steak and pound well with the back of a large
wooden spoon, sprinkling it with about ½ cup of flour,
pounding it well into it. Put the steak in a frying-pan and
brown on both sides. When nicely browned, cover with
boiling water, add 4 or 5 sliced onions, pepper and salt, and
simmer for 2 hours, adding a little more water if necessary.

From Miss W. Palmer, Stanford Farm, Old Buckenham, Norwich.

TRANSVAAL ROAST

THIS is a far more interesting way of cooking breast of
mutton than stewing it, and is moreover delicious when cold,
and very economical. Buy the meat ready boned (the butcher
does it much better than oneself). See that you have the bones,
though, for gravy. For 2 cups of breadcrumbs, take ¾ teaspoonful of salt, a good dash of pepper, a finely-chopped onion, 1 level
tablespoonful (not more) each of dried parsley (or fresh) and
thyme. Mix well with 2 eggs. Open the meat, spread it
evenly with the stuffing, roll and tie tightly. If you can bake it
in a pie-dish, just to fit, so much the better. Baste well and cook
slowly for at least 2 hours. Serve with apple jelly and the
usual gravy and vegetables.

From Mrs. W. Levers, P.O. Boskop Rail, Transvaal, South Africa.

STUFFED LOIN OF LAMB

GET your butcher to bone a loin of lamb before sending it.
Then mix together 3 ozs. breadcrumbs, 1½ ozs. shredded
suet, ½ teaspoonful of mixed herbs, a little grated lemon rind, 1
small teaspoonful of chopped parsley and seasoning. Mix
together into a crumbly paste with beaten egg. Put this into the
loin where the bone was removed, roll the meat round and tie
firmly with tape in several places. Roast for 1 hour 20 minutes.

To serve, cut in neat slices and arrange in the centre of a hot
dish. Put little heaps of vegetables round: green peas, potatoes
and asparagus look very attractive.

From Mrs. Bartlett, Parsonage, Watchet, Somerset.

SPRING LAMB

PUT 2 cupfuls of fine breadcrumbs into a basin, add 2 tablespoonfuls shredded suet, 2 teaspoonfuls chopped mint,
seasoning of salt and pepper. Mix with a beaten egg and a
little milk.

Have the bone taken out of a shoulder of lamb. Well skewer the shoulder after the stuffing has been put in. Dredge the outer skin with flour, put 2 or 3 knobs of dripping on top, and roast in a hot oven for 1½ hours.

From Miss F. Smithson, Boston Road Dairy, Donington, Spalding, Lincs.

CALF'S HEAD PIE

BOIL a calf's head till tender, then cut off the meat in thin slices. Make some good stock of the bones, skimming it carefully and flavouring with vegetables, herbs, etc. Next day make the pie.

Take some slices of hard-boiled eggs and lay them in the bottom of a greased pie-dish, and on these put alternate layers of meat and jelly, more eggs, and so on. Flavour all delicately till the dish is full.

Cover with some good puff paste and bake till the pastry is quite done. When cold, carefully remove the pastry and turn it upside-down on a cold dish and turn the contents of the pie on to it. This makes quite a pretty mould, and is very tasty.

From Miss A. Harrison, Yew Tree Farm, Toby's Hill, Draycott-in-the-Clay,
Sudbury, Derby.

BACON IN CIDER

IN Sussex I was shown the following way of cooking bacon. It is delicious. You will want 1 corner bacon (6 lbs.), 1 pint cider, 1 bunch sweet herbs, 1 dozen cloves, 1 teacupful brown breadcrumbs and 2 ozs. brown sugar.

Soak bacon overnight. Then bring to the boil, pour off water and add fresh. Add herbs and simmer slowly, allowing 20 minutes to each pound, and pouring in the cider 1 hour before it is done. When cooked, let ham cool and remove skin; cover with sugar and breadcrumbs, and stick with cloves. Bake till brown.

From Miss Nellie Richmond, Ballytaggart, Ballymoney, Co. Antrim.

PIG'S HEAD PUDDING

½ pig's head.	½ lb. breadcrumbs.
3 eggs.	½ nutmeg.
Any available cooked beef.	Pepper.

SOAK the head, nose and ears overnight; having first soaked them in salt for a fortnight or more. Then boil for 2½ hours. When cold, put through a mincer with the cooked beef. Add

B

the grated nutmeg, breadcrumbs and pepper to taste. Then mix in the eggs and make it into a firm roll. Tie in a pudding cloth like a roly-poly; place in boiling water, and boil for 2 hours. Serve cold.

From Mrs. Parsons, Illand, Congdonshop, Launceston, Cornwall.

PIG'S FEET AND PARSLEY SAUCE

WASH thoroughly 4 pigs' feet. Put them in a saucepan with enough water to cover. Bring to the boil, skim, and simmer gently for 2½ hours.

Make a parsley sauce with ½ pint milk, 1 tablespoonful chopped parsley, 1 tablespoonful cornflour (or plain flour), a piece of butter or margarine, salt and pepper. Serve with the pigs' feet. This is sufficient for 6 people.

A good soup can be made with the addition of vegetables to the stock in which the feet were boiled.

From Mrs. G. E. Jones, Lower House Farm, Eastmeon, Petersfield.

PORK CHEESE

IN Scotland we are very fond of cold meats and brawns for Sunday supper, and this is a nice dish which is always a favourite.

Chop coarsely 1 lb. of lean pork and 1 lb. of inside fat. Strew over and thoroughly mix in 3 teaspoonfuls of salt, half as much pepper, 1 teaspoonful of finely-chopped parsley, thyme and sage (mixed), and 1 tablespoonful of chopped chives, or spring onions.

Press the meat closely and evenly into a shallow tin, such as we use for a Yorkshire pudding, and bake in a gentle oven for 1 hour. When done, pour over ½ pint of aspic jelly that has been made with some well-seasoned bone stock. Allow to set, then serve the pork cheese cold, in slices, with a green salad. Minced mushrooms are very nice added to the pork, when they are available.

From Mrs. R. Johnstone, The Linkins, Castle Douglas, Kircudbright, Scotland.

IMITATION JUGGED HARE

A GOOD imitation of jugged hare can be made with shin of beef. Cut the meat into slices about the size of the joints of a hare, flour well and just fry brown in a little dripping. Place in a casserole with an onion stuck with four cloves, a strip of lemon rind, a teaspoonful of mixed herbs and seasoning. Cook slowly for 3 hours. When finished, strain the gravy and thicken with 1 teaspoonful of flour mixed with a little ketchup. Put meat on hot dish and pour gravy over. If served with redcurrant jelly and forcemeat balls the illusion is complete.

For forcemeat balls, mix 2 tablespoonsful breadcrumbs, ½ oz. butter or chopped suet, ½ teaspoonful parsley and herbs, ¼ teaspoonful grated lemon rind, seasoning, 1 beaten egg to mix. Roll into balls and " poach " in boiling water 10 minutes. These are much more wholesome than fried, and should be laid round the dish.

From Mrs. A. E. Godfrey, Rackstraw Farm, Camberley, Surrey.

SAVOURY MUTTON PIE

2 lbs. fillet mutton.
4 tomatoes.
1 large onion.

1 lb. sausage.
1 teaspoonful barley.
Salt and pepper.

For the crust:

1 lb. flour.
½ lb. lard.

1 teaspoonful baking powder.

LAY mutton flat in saucepan and cover with water. Add barley, onion (chopped), salt and pepper to taste. Simmer till tender, then lift it bodily into a pie-dish with some gravy. Next fry the sausages gently and drain on to greaseproof paper for 2 minutes, and lay round the mutton. Place a tomato in each corner.

For pie crust, put flour into a warm bowl, add salt and 1 teaspoonful of baking powder and mix well. Rub half the lard into flour and make up the pastry with water. Roll out flat. Divide remaining lard into 3 portions. Take 1 portion and with the end of a knife distribute in small portions at equal distances over pastry. Fold over 4 times and roll out again. Repeat this twice more and then place pastry on pie and bake in a hot oven for 40 minutes.

From Miss M. Scott, Broats Farm, Pickering.

LIVER IN BATTER

LIVER cooked in this way makes it as tender as chicken. Take about ½ lb. liver, cut it in small portions, make a batter of 2 tablespoons of self-raising flour, a pinch of salt and cold water. Have ready a pan of boiling fat, dip each piece of liver in the batter, and fry till a nice golden brown. Serve hot with vegetables.

From Miss W. Palmer, Staxford Farm, Old Buckenham, Norwich.

ROAST LIVER

YOU will be surprised to discover how good roast liver is. Have 1 lb. cut off in a solid piece. Ask the butcher to gash it in the centre, almost through to the other side, so as to make a sort of pocket. Stuff this with a dressing made by chopping a thin rasher of bacon and 1 onion, and mixing them with breadcrumbs, 1 egg well beaten, and enough hot water to moisten the crumbs. Tie a string round the liver to hold it together, lard it with thin rashers of bacon, and bake until tender. Make a brown gravy with the fat in the baking dish. Serve with currant jelly.

From Mrs. A. E. Godfrey, Rackstraw Farm, Camberley, Surrey.

LIVER AND BACON HOT-POT

1 lb. pig's liver.   Breadcrumbs.
Salt and pepper.   Onions.
½ lb. streaky bacon.   Chopped parsley and marjoram.
Apples.

CHOP the apples and onions, cut bacon in very thin slices and liver in thin pieces. Place a layer of liver in a greased casserole or pie-dish, cover with bacon, sprinkle with breadcrumbs, parsley, onions, marjoram, salt and pepper. Add one thick layer of chopped, sharp apples. Repeat these layers until dish is full, the last layer being breadcrumbs; fill dish right up with lukewarm water. Bake in a moderately hot oven for 2 hours, covering the dish. Add a little more water if it gets too dry. ½ hour before the cooking is finished, remove the cover to brown top. Serve very hot.

From Mrs. Doris Vincent, Pound Lane, Up-Ottery, near Honiton, Devon.

OLD DERBYSHIRE CURED HAM
(*For a ham weighing* 10-12 *lbs.*)

1 pint old ale.
1 pint of stout.
¾ lb. treacle.

¾ bag salt.
¾ lb. coarse salt.
¼ oz. saltpetre.

PUT into a saucepan the ingredients, boil for about 5 minutes. While the mixture is boiling, rub the ham with coarse salt and put it in a large pickling pan. Then pour over the mixture while it is hot. Keep the ham in pickle for 3 weeks, turning and rubbing it every day. After this, take out, put it into a thin cotton bag, and hang it up in the kitchen.

From Mrs. M. Johnson, Nottinghamshire.

COOKING A HAM
(*An Economical Method*)

PUT your ham in the copper, well cover with cold water, and slowly bring to boil. Boil for 20 minutes, if ham is 15 lbs. or under; for 20 lbs. or more, 1 hour is sufficient. Then take away all fire from underneath and well cover the copper with old coats, bags or anything to keep in the heat. Leave for about 12 hours (if cooked overnight leave until next morning). Lift off coats, etc., also cover, and if water is cold enough, lift ham on dish. You will have a well-cooked but not over-cooked ham with a minimum amount of fuel.

From Mrs. M. Francis, Phippens Farm, Stoke St. Michael, Oakhill, near Bath.

ELIZABETH PASTY

LINE a fairly deep tin or plate with pastry and fill with the following mixture :

Take of the " scratchings " left over from lard making about 1 lb., the tongue of the pig, the heart, and about 8 ozs. of liver, which must be rather more than half boiled ; 1 small teacupful of well-washed currants ; 1 teaspoonful of chopped mixed herbs ; 1 onion, which must be part boiled, and cut in rings, not chopped ; salt and pepper as liked ; 1 teaspoonful Demerara sugar ; 2 ozs. breadcrumbs ; 2 hard-boiled eggs.

Place part of the " scratchings " smoothly on the bottom of the pastry in the tin, then cut tongue, liver and heart in slices ; place on top the mixed breadcrumbs and sugar, currants and herbs, together with a little stock (in which tongue, etc., was cooked) ; spread this smoothly over meat, season well, place alternate rings of onion and hard-boiled egg on top, taking care not to separate the yolk from the white; cover with the remainder of the " scratchings " and pastry and bake in a medium oven until thoroughly cooked—about 1 hour.

This old recipe was given me some years ago by an old Herefordshire lady, and it has been used by her family for several generations, handed down from mother to daughter. I have never seen it published in any book or magazine.

From Mrs. F. Preston, Oxfordshire.

PORK PIE

3½ lbs. flour, heated quite hot.
1 lb. lard.

1 pint water.
½ teaspoonful of salt.

For the filling:

3 lbs. pork (2 parts lean and 1 part fat) cut very small and well mixed.

1 oz. salt.
1 teaspoonful of anchovy essence or sauce.

THIS is a recipe that has been in my family for over a century, and at Christmas time is very much sought after, having a most subtle flavour.

Boil lard, water and salt together. Pour over the heated flour and mix with a wooden spoon. When cool enough to handle, knead well for 15 minutes. If you have no mould, a 2-lb. jar will do to shape the pastry. When set, take off the mould and fill, packing the meat well to form a good shape when baking.

Fasten a band of greaseproof paper around the pastry, fix on a pastry lid and decorate with fancy shape in bold design, leaves, etc. Make centre hole and bake for 2½ hours in a hot oven first, then moderate the heat to finish. Make your jelly by stewing the gristle and pig's foot. Pour a little into the pie when baked. This will make a good family-size pie or two smaller ones. *From Mrs. M. Hemsley, Morton, Newark, Notts.*

BACON AND EGG PIE

Cooked ham or bacon.
Eggs.

Flaky pastry.

LINE a shallow dish with flaky pastry. Spread a layer of cooked ham or bacon on it, and then break the eggs over the meat, so that the whites of the eggs run together, and the yolks are placed evenly apart. Cover the whole with another thin layer of pastry, and bake in a moderate oven for about ½ hour. *From Marjorie H. Bosley, Berkshire.*

VEAL AND HAM PIE

1 lb. filleted veal.
¼ lb. ham.
2 hard-boiled eggs.
1 teaspoonful chopped parsley.

½ teaspoonful herbs.
A little grated lemon rind.
Salt and pepper.
Stock.

For the pastry:

10 ozs. flour.
6 ozs. butter and lard mixed.

Water to mix.
Egg to glaze.

COOK the veal in enough cold water to cover, with an onion stuck with 2 cloves. When cold, cut into thin slices, put a pinch of seasoning (parsley, herbs, lemon peel, salt and pepper) on each slice and roll up. Pack the rolls in a pie-dish, not too tightly, with the ham and hard-boiled eggs cut in slices. Reduce the stock, adding a leaf of gelatine if necessary, and pour it into the pie-dish.

Cover with pastry, decorate with leaves and a rose, brush over with egg, bake for 1½ to 1¾ hours, remove the rose and pour in the remainder of the stock through the hole. Rough puff or flaky pastry can be used for this dish. This is a very old recipe which can be recommended.

From Mrs. F. Mayne, Wingroad Farm, Stewkley, Leighton Buzzard, Beds.

HUNTINGDON FIDGET PIE

1 lb. cooking apples.
½ lb. onions.
¾ lb. streaky, home-cured bacon.

Seasoning.
Pastry crust.

PUT 1 layer of apples at the bottom of a pie-dish, on top of this place a layer of sliced onions, followed by a layer of bacon cut into dice. Repeat until dish is full, adding to each layer a sprinkling of pepper and salt. Add a very little water, cover with a good pastry crust, and bake in a moderate oven for 2 hours.

From Mrs. D. Berry, Huntingdon.

GAMMON AND APRICOT PIE

1 gammon rasher 1 in. thick.
½ lb. dried apricots.
Pepper.

1 oz. sultanas.
6 potatoes.
A little gravy.

LIGHTLY brown the rasher on both sides in a frying-pan. Lay in a large pie-dish. Place apricots—which have been in water 12 hours previously—on top. Sprinkle a little pepper over, add the sultanas, pour a little gravy over, cover with sliced potatoes. Put a piece of greaseproof paper over all and bake in a moderate oven for 1 hour. Serve hot.

From Miss E. Hughes, Aylesbury, Bucks.

MARKET DAY SAVOURY

THIS can be left cooking on an oil stove while you go to market. Take 6 small pork chops, 2 pig's kidneys, 1 lb. onions, 1½ lbs. potatoes, 1 small apple, 1 teaspoonful dried sage, 1 tablespoonful tomato sauce. Peel and slice potatoes and onions, put in a stew jar in layers with the chops and sliced kidneys. Sprinkle sliced onion, apple and seasoning among them. Cover with a layer of potatoes. Pour over a teacupful of water, put on a tight-fitting lid and cook slowly for 2 or 3 hours. The longer you cook this dish the more savoury it will be.

From Mrs. M. Arundel, Kirby Bellars, Melton Mowbray. Leics.

STUFFED CHINE

Chine.	Marjoram.
Parsley.	Mace.
Leeks (or chives).	Salt.

SOAK the chine one night in water, having first weighed it. Wipe dry, then cut well into the bone, across both sides. Mix up stuffing made of the other ingredients, press it well into each slit : tie in a clean cloth and boil ; allowing ½ hour for the first pound and ¼ hour for each other pound.

This was always prepared for suppers, and was called " the sheep-shearing chine." It was taken from the back of a big fat pig. My grandmother used this recipe when she was young. She has been dead about thirty-five years, and she was nearly 75 when she died.

From Mrs. M. Bloxham, Warwickshire.

PORK PUDDING

1 lb. flour.	½ lb. salt pork (fat).
¾ lb. raisins.	A little salt.

CHOP up the pork, but not too finely, and mix with the flour and a little salt ; then add the raisins, previously stoned, and mix all to a stiff batter with milk. Put into a well-greased baking tin, and bake until well cooked. An egg may be added if you have one to spare.

From Mrs. E. M., Bromley, Kent.

SWEET PICKLED PORK

One small leg or a small hand of pork.
3 ozs. coarse salt.
3 ozs. bay salt.
½ oz. saltpetre.
½ pint ale.
½ pint stout.

PUT the leg or hand of pork in a crock, after rubbing it well with coarse salt. Break up fine 3 ozs. of coarse salt, 3 ozs. of bay salt, and the ½ oz. of saltpetre, and mix the three together. Put them into a saucepan with the ale and the stout, bring to the boil, stirring often: and pour the mixture over the pork, boiling hot. Turn the pork over in the pickle every day for 14 days. It is then ready to cook—and it may be either boiled or baked and is delicious hot or cold.

From Mrs. A. Shute, Wootton Fitzpaine, Dorset.

TURKEY PORK

A leg of pork.
Flour.
Dripping.
Forcemeat balls.
Bread sauce.

COOKED in the following way a leg of pork will taste like turkey. Take off the skin and bone the leg ; make a plain crust with the flour and dripping, roll out very thin, and fold the pork in it. Bake it in a moderate oven ; allowing 25 minutes to each pound of pork. Break off the crust ; and you will find your pork beautifully white and tender. Serve with brown gravy, forcemeat balls and bread sauce. Cut the crust into neat pieces and serve on a separate dish. *From Mrs. C. Ball, Bedfordshire.*

SWEDES WITH BACON

TAKE thin slices of smoked bacon and put a layer in the bottom of a saucepan, then a layer of swede turnip, and so on, in alternate layers till you have as much as required. Then add 2 tablespoonfuls of cold water and place at side of stove and simmer gently till cooked. The swedes stew in their own liquid and absorb the flavour of the bacon, and in consequence are altogether more delicious than when cooked in the usual way.

From Miss K. Murphy, Bishopstown, Carrigrohane, Cork.

WHITE PUDDINGS

THIS recipe for " White Puddings " was always used at pig-killing times in a Northumbrian farmhouse of last century. Take half a pig's head, brain, tongue, lights, heart, kidneys and rinds, also any odd pieces of pork. Boil together all except brain and rinds. Boil brain separately in a piece of muslin. When well cooked take meat from bones, and pass all through a mincer. Boil ¼ lb. pearl barley and add to other ingredients. Mix well together and season with salt and pepper. Use stock from boiling to moisten, but do not make too damp. Fill well-scraped skins and fry in a little lard.

From Mrs. M. J. Wilson, Hill Farm, Gestingthorpe, Castle Hedingham, Essex.

BLACK PUDDINGS

1 quart of fresh pig's blood.
1 quart of new or skimmed milk.
½ loaf of bread cut into cubes.
1 cup of rice.

1 cup of barley.
1 lb. fresh beef suet.
2 or 3 handfuls dry oatmeal.
Pepper, salt, black pepper and dried mint.

PLACE the bread in a large pie-dish ; pour the milk over this, and set in the oven to warm gently. Do not make too hot. Have ready the blood in a large bowl, and pour into this the milk and bread when warm. Prepare the rice and barley beforehand by bursting with water and cooking well in the oven. Add this to the blood as well. Then grate into this the beef suet, stirring up with the oatmeal. Season with the pepper, salt, black pepper and dried mint. Put into well-greased dripping-pans about three-quarters full, and bake in a moderate oven until cooked through.

This is much easier for the busy farmwife than filling into skins. When warmed up in the frying-pan or oven they last quite a long while and are grand for breakfast or supper. They are even eaten for dinner with mashed potatoes up north. These puddings are always delicious, and as light as a feather.

From Mrs. M. E. Glover, Westmorland.

QUORN BACON ROLL

THIS is a dish for a cold day, very popular in the Quorn country.

Make a suet paste with equal quantities of flour and shredded suet, a pinch of salt and enough water to moisten. Roll out, about ¼ in. thick. Lay rashers of lean bacon—collar is best—on the paste, and sprinkle with sage and chopped onion. Roll up, wrap in a pudding cloth and boil for about 2 hours. (Allow about ½ lb. bacon for 3 people.) Serve on a hot dish, sprinkled with chopped parsley and surrounded with potatoes, carrots and turnips. *Miss Peggy Crawford, Caudale Farm, Lowesby, near Leicester.*

WILTSHIRE PORKIES

M IX ¼ lb. flour with ½ teaspoonful salt in a basin, add the
yolk of 1 egg, 1 tablespoonful salad oil and enough water
to make a batter which will coat the back of a spoon. Beat well
and let it stand for ½ hour. Form 1 lb. sausage meat into
small, neat rolls, flouring the hands and board to prevent sticking. Whisk the white of the egg stiffly, stir into the batter, then
coat each roll with batter and fry in deep, boiling fat until
brown. Pile on a hot dish and serve with apple rings fried in the
batter. Garnish with fried parsley.

From Mrs. C. Gibbons, Poynton, Cheshire.

STUFFED SUMMER CABBAGE

1 cabbage.
1 lb. minced pork (lean).
2 ozs. butter.
¼ lb. whole rice.
1 onion.
1 egg.

S EPARATE leaves of cabbage, keeping larger leaves whole for
stuffing. Mince remainder of cabbage finely and boil in
salted water for 8 minutes, allowing to steam for 8 minutes
longer with lid on pan. Strain cabbage thoroughly. Grease
pan and put layer of minced cabbage on bottom, then fill each
large leaf with stuffing and lay on top, covering all with remainder of cabbage and small nuts of butter.

Prepare stuffing thus : Mix minced meat with rice previously
boiled, and egg (not beaten), onion finely minced with salt and
pepper to taste. Stew slowly for 1½ hours.

From Mrs. Cromar, Tillychardoch, Tarland, Aberdeenshire.

BUCKINGHAMSHIRE DUMPLING

1 lb. flour.
6 ozs. suet.
½ lb. fat bacon, cut into thin strips.
½ lb. liver cut small.
2 large onions, grated.
1 dessertspoonful of chopped sage.
Salt and pepper to taste.

M IX the flour and suet into a stiff dough, adding a little salt ;
roll out on a floured paste-board. Cover the dough with
the cut-up bacon. Now cover the bacon with the small pieces
of liver, spread over with the grated onion and chopped sage ;
add pepper and salt. Roll up tightly in a floured cloth and boil
about 2½ hours.

Serve with a good brown gravy made from a pint of stock
and a little beef extract : thicken with a tablespoonful of cornflour, stirring all the time for 5 minutes to keep it smooth.

From Mrs. E. A. Hurst, Leckhampstead, Buckingham.

POTATO, HAM AND CHEESE PASTY

¼ lb. fat ham.
¼ lb. mashed potatoes.
1 large onion.

2 ozs. cheese.
4 sage leaves.
Pepper and salt.

MAKE an ordinary pastry crust of ½ lb. self-raising flour and ¼ lb. lard, water and salt, and roll out flat on the board. Cut the ham into small squares, grate the cheese and cut the onion into strips. Cut the sage leaves finely, have the potatoes mashed ready and mix with the other ingredients. Add the pepper and salt to taste. Put on to the pastry, wet the edges all round and press together. Put on a greased baking-tin, and bake for 1 hour in a moderate oven. This is vey nice hot or cold.

From Mrs. E. Macey, Harmlake Farm, Sutton Valence, Kent.

CORNISH PASTY

½ lb. flour.
⅓ lb. steak.
¼ lb. butter.
2 medium-sized potatoes.

1 small onion.
Salt and pepper.
A little cold water.

RUB the fat into the flour, add the salt and mix into a stiff dough with the water. Divide into two parts and roll each piece out thinly into a round. Season the chopped potatoes, onion and sliced meat, mix and place a layer on one half of each piece of pastry. Fold over the other half and pinch together. Bake in a moderate oven for ¾ hour. This is sufficient for 2 pasties.

From Miss V. Newton, Rees Farm, Callestick, Truro, Cornwall.

TOAD SPECIAL

FIRST make a batter with 2 eggs, 5 ozs. flour, a pinch of salt, tablespoonful water and sufficient milk to make to a thick, creamy consistency. Allow this to stand 1 hour or longer. In well-greased flat fireproof dish lay tiny rolls of thinly-cut veal, stuffed with breadcrumbs, parsley, milk and seasoning and a quarter slice of a rasher of bacon. Pour the batter over the neatly arranged rolls, and cook for ½ to ¾ hour in a moderate to hot oven. Ornament the top, when nearly cooked, with cooked mushrooms or uncooked slices of tomato. This is a good way of using up remains of a joint.

From Mrs. Kitchener, Olney, Bucks.

DUTCH ROLL

½ lb. cold meat.
1 thick slice stale bread.
¼ pint gravy or milk.
Salt.

¼ lb. mashed potatoes.
1 teaspoonful chopped onion.
Browned breadcrumbs.
Pepper.

BREAK the bread into small pieces, soak them in the gravy or milk, beat out all the lumps with a fork, and add the finely-chopped meat. Add the potato, onion and salt and pepper to taste, and mix all well together. Grease a basin or mould, coat it thickly with browned breadcrumbs, and pour in the mixture. Press it down firmly with a greased paper, and either steam or bake gently for about 1 hour.

From Mrs. Smith, Hampton, Worcestershire.

MEAT PUFFS

2 ozs. breadcrumbs.
1 lb. mashed potatoes.
2 ozs. flour.
2 eggs.

1 oz. butter.
minced cold meat.
Pepper and salt.

THIS is to use up left-overs of meat, bread and potatoes.

First mash the potatoes, then add butter, breadcrumbs, flour and seasoning, and last of all 1 egg well beaten. Make this into a paste, dredge with flour and roll out. Cut into squares about ¼ in. thick and fill these with minced meat. Fold over corner ways, egg and breadcrumb the rolls, shake off all the loose crumbs, and fry a rich brown. Serve with a good gravy.

From Mrs. G. Carnell, Besthorpe, near Newark, Notts.

TRIPE WITH TOMATOES

THIS is a good spring dish, and one which all tripe eaters may like to try. You will need 2 lbs. of tripe, a bunch of herbs, 1 lb. of tomatoes, 2 onions, 2 ozs. of dripping, pepper, salt and 1 large tablespoonful of flour.

First, cut up the tripe and blanch it. Fry the herbs and sliced onions in the fat, and when browned a little, stir in the flour. Pass the tomatoes through a sieve, put into the stew-pan with the onions, etc., and stir till very hot. Add the tripe to the sauce ; season all, and simmer slowly for 1½ hours. Chop some parsley very finely and scatter over all. Have fried pieces of bread for a further garnish.

From Mrs. A. D. Jones, Cheshire.

SCALLOPED MEAT WITH MACARONI

2 cupfuls tomato soup or gravy.
1 cupful cooked macaroni.
2 cupfuls cooked meat (chopped).

1 cupful browned breadcrumbs.
Salt and pepper to taste.
Butter.

ARRANGE the cooked macaroni, meat and gravy in alternate layers in a casserole. Sprinkle each layer with salt and pepper, cover the top with browned breadcrumbs. Dot with butter and bake in moderate oven until mixture is heated through.

From Miss L. Pound, Kent.

MEAT ROLY-POLY

$\frac{3}{4}$ lb. self-raising flour.
6 ozs. chopped suet.
$\frac{1}{2}$ lb. any cold roast meat, minced.
2 large onions, minced.

$\frac{1}{2}$ teaspoonful salt.
$\frac{1}{4}$ teaspoonful pepper.
$\frac{1}{2}$ pint good gravy.

MAKE suet crust with flour, suet and water. Roll out $\frac{1}{2}$ in. thick. Mix together the chopped onion and minced meat, season well and spread over the pastry. Wet the edges and roll up. Press the ends before covering with a scalded and floured pudding cloth. Place in pan of boiling water. Boil for 2 hours.

From Mrs. Edith Williams, Monmouthshire.

TINNED CORNED BEEF HASH

8 ozs. corned beef.
4 ozs. large or haricot beans (soaked overnight).
2 dessertspoonfuls of pearl barley.
1 beef cube (crushed).
2 onions, cut small.

1 carrot thinly sliced.
2 ozs. turnip or swede cut into 1 in. cubes.
$\frac{1}{2}$ bay leaf (optional).
Salt and pepper to taste, preferably gravy salt.

RINSE the beans and place in pan along with all the other items except the corned beef. Well cover them with heated stock or boiling water, and boil slowly until the beans are cooked, stirring occasionally. Then add the beef cut into small pieces, and thicken the hash with a little flour ; heat through.

This recipe can be varied by adding soaked peas in place of beans and pearl barley, and using dried mint to flavour in place of bay leaf. The following vegetables boiled or steamed together make an unusual but tasty accompaniment to the above-mentioned dishes : 1 medium-sized onion, 2 carrots, $\frac{1}{2}$ a small swede or 2 turnips, all sliced small, put in a pan with 4 large potatoes left whole. When cooked, drain well and dry a little, add seasoning to taste and a little butter, and mash well together. Sufficient for 4 persons.

From Mrs. E. W. Anderson, Hipperholme, near Halifax.

MUTTON AND PICKLE DISH

Cold mutton.   Salt and pepper.
Gravy.   Breadcrumbs.
3 pickled walnuts.   3 large pickled onions.

PUT some cold mutton in slices, sprinkle with salt and pepper.
Dip the slices first in gravy, then in breadcrumbs, and put
into a greased pie-dish. Chop finely the pickled walnuts and
pickled onions. Spread a layer of pickles over the meat, add a
spoonful of liquor from the pickles, then another layer of
mutton and pickles. Set the dish in the oven to get thoroughly
hot, put some snippets of toasted bread on top and serve.

From Miss A. E. Parry, Flintshire.

GRANNY MORGAN'S BRAWN

CLEAN a pig's head and soak in brine for a few days. Before
using, wash in clean cold water. Boil until the meat drops
from the bone. In a separate saucepan cook the liver, heart and
tongue, until very tender. Strain the stock in which the head
was cooked, then turn this stock into that in which the remainder
of the meat was cooked ; add to it 6 black peppercorns, and an
equal number of whole cloves, and boil until it is reduced to
1 pint. Strain again, add 1 cupful of good vinegar and re-heat.
In the meantime, chop the meat or put it through the mincer,
add seasoning of chopped onions or sage if desired. Add
salt and pepper if needed. Pack into stone crocks, pour the
stock over it, cover with a plate, weight well, cover with a
cloth and set aside for a week before using.

From Mrs. Jones, Nanthirwen, Moelfre, Oswestry.

PRESSED BEEF

3 lbs. of brisket or flat ribs of beef.   1 meat cube.
½ cow's heel.

PUT these into a saucepan with seasoning and enough cold
water nearly to cover the beef. Let the water come to the
boil and draw the saucepan on to the side of the fire and let the
water simmer for 2½ hours. Now lift out beef, remove bones
carefully, and put it into a pudding-dish. Sprinkle a little salt
over to taste and pour over some of the liquid. Then put a plate
on the top and weight down. Leave until next day, then turn
out. The beef will be covered with brown jelly.

From Mrs. M. Rogers, Wrexham.

CHRISTMAS SPICED BEEF

For about 15 *lbs. of beef (boneless meat is best)*

1 oz. bay salt.	½ oz. cloves.
8 ozs. Demerara sugar.	2 ozs. black pepper.
¼ oz. Jamaica pepper.	Salt.
1 oz. saltpetre.	

RUB the beef well with sugar, bay salt, salt and saltpetre. Then cover with the peppers, and stick the cloves in the meat. Let it stand for about 3 weeks, turning and basting every day. Before cooking take out the cloves and roast in the usual way.

From Mrs. H. Jarvis, Eakley Lanes, Stoke Goldington, near Bletchley.

HARVEST-TIME MOULD

1 cow's heel, or 2 pig's feet.	Cut vegetables.
1 lb. of shoulder steak.	Pepper.
Ham scraps.	Salt.

STEW the cow's heel or pig's feet very slowly with the shoulder steak and ham scraps. Season with pepper and salt, and add the vegetables. When thoroughly well cooked cut up the meat into small pieces, and pour with the liquor into a mould that has been well rinsed in cold water. Then leave to set, and turn out next day. This is excellent served with a nice green salad and a few cut hard-boiled eggs, making quite a good meal if all have been out in the fields during the day.

This dish is economical and easily prepared—which is what we require in these days when, as farmers' wives, it is necessary to consider expenses and our time.

From Mrs. H. M. Dimmond, Worcestershire.

ABBEY FARM BRAWN

TAKE ½ a pig's head, which has been salted for 3 or 4 days. Soak for 1 or 2 hours in water and wash all the salt off. Cook gently in just enough water to cover, with a few peppercorns added, until the meat can be slipped easily from the bones. Remove the rough skin (the fine skin may be left on, particularly if it is a young pig) ; and skin the tongue.

At the same time, but in a separate receptacle, cook an old fowl—no matter how old—in water to which has been added 1 medium-sized onion, 1 or 2 leaves of parsley, 1 small teaspoonful of salt, ½ teaspoonful of pepper and the giblets. Boil very gently until the bird is thoroughly tender ; and while still warm, cut up the meat in neat slices, removing all the bones, and using the breast meat to place in the bottom and sides of the moulds or pie-dishes.

Place a layer of pig meat next, and alternate with fowl until all the meat is used up; seasoning with pepper to taste between the rows. This quantity makes 2 large pie-dishes or 3 moulds. Mix the 2 liquors the meats have been cooked in, and strain it —this will make a clear jelly—and with it fill up the dishes and leave in a cool place to set.

The secret of the goodness of this dish, and the attractive appearance, lies in the very slow cooking (so that the meat has no trace of "ragginess"): and in the separate cooking of the meat to retain the distinct red and white flesh.

From Mrs. C. Harrison, Abbey Farm, Renhold, Beds.

MEAT LOAF

1½ lbs. neck of beef.	¼ teaspoonful paprika.
¼ lb. fresh pork from shoulder.	½ cupful canned tomatoes.
½ cupful breadcrumbs, soaked in milk or water.	⅛ teaspoonful celery salt.
	Dash of black pepper.
1 tablespoonful minced parsley.	1 tablespoonful grated onion.
1¼ teaspoonfuls salt.	

RUN the meat through the mincer, and let it remain on a plate for 1 hour or longer. Then add the soaked breadcrumbs, tomato, onion, parsley and celery salt and seasoning. Mix thoroughly, shape into a loaf, or press into a greased baking-tin (deep). Brush with beaten egg, sprinkle with crumbs, and bake 1½ hours in a moderate oven. Baste with melted butter or bacon dripping and hot water. Serve with tomato sauce.

From Dorothy Alder, Shropshire.

LAMB MOULD

DISSOLVE ½ oz. gelatine in ½ pint of hot water, add 1 tea-spoonful lemon juice, 2 dessertspoonfuls of castor sugar, 1 teaspoonful of salt, and ½ gill of vinegar. Strain, and allow to cool. As soon as it begins to set add 1¼ gills finely-shredded cabbage, 1 tablespoonful cooked peas, 1 sliced hard-boiled egg, and diced or sliced lamb to taste.

Turn into a wet mould and leave until set. Serve turned out on a bed of lettuce leaves, accompanied by mayonnaise and tomatoes.

From Mrs. A. M. Duckett, The Poplars, Keinton-Mandeville, Taunton.

SAVOURY AND MEATLESS DISHES

SAVOURY SCRAMBLED EGGS

Butter.   Onion.
3 eggs.   Chopped parsley.
Pepper and salt.

MELT a piece of butter in a pan, pour into it 3 well-beaten eggs seasoned with pepper and salt; also a little braised onion and chopped parsley. Cook, stirring all the time with a fork, until set. Serve on hot buttered toast. A little mushroom sauce may be sprinkled on top.

From Mrs. A. E. Clamp, West Bridgford, Notts.

EGG PUFFS

HALVE some hard-boiled eggs lengthwise. Dip them in melted butter on a plate, and sprinkle them with a mixture of finely-chopped parsley, a little lemon thyme, grated lemon rind, a few chopped capers, a pinch of nutmeg, pepper and salt. Then roll out some scraps of pastry very thinly and cut out two ovals for each half egg. Place one under and one over each piece, and pinch the edges together.

Brush the puffs over with a little milk or beaten egg, and sprinkle them with finely-grated cheese. Bake in a good oven until brown and crisp. These are good for high tea or supper.

From Mrs. Roberts, Coedlan Farm, Llanfyllin, Mont.

EGG TOAST

BEAT up the eggs with a little milk and salt, as if for scrambled eggs. Cut the bread as if for toast and soak both sides in the egg till the bread is saturated. Fry in hot fat till a golden brown on both sides. Serve plain or with either jam or sugar to taste.

From Miss O. M. Montgomery, Winford Manor, near Bristol, Somerset.

EGG PIE

GREASE a pie-dish, line it with fine crumbs, season with pepper and salt. Cover with a layer of tomatoes, then a thin layer of mashed potatoes. On to this break 4 or 5 eggs, according to the size of your dish. Scatter chopped gherkins or capers lightly over; then add some breadcrumbs, another layer of tomatoes, and so on until the dish is full. Let the last layer be breadcrumbs. Place a few bits of butter on top and bake about 20 minutes. *From Mrs. Rogers, Acton Park, Wrexham.*

SAVOURY NUT PUDDING

3 large potatoes.	1 tablespoonful grated cheese.
2 oz. mixed nuts.	½ cupful milk.
1 oz. butter.	Pepper, salt and nutmeg.
1 egg.	

WASH the potatoes and bake in a moderate oven until tender. Remove the skins and press potatoes through a sieve. Melt butter in a saucepan, add the sieved potato, stir in the milk, and season. Add the nuts, chopped small, and the yolk of the egg; mixing with beaten white of egg. Put in a buttered pie-dish, sprinkle the grated cheese over the top, stand in a moderate oven and bake until brown.

From Mrs. M. E. Taylor, Buckinghamshire.

SAVOURY RICE

4 eggs.	1 tablespoonful chopped raisins.
4 ozs. rice.	1 oz. grated Parmesan cheese.
2 ozs. butter.	2 tablespoonfuls tomato sauce.
1 pint stock.	Salt, pepper and paprika.
1 teaspoonful lemon juice.	1 teaspoonful chopped parsley.
3 shallots.	

MELT the butter in a stew-pan, add well-washed rice and finely-chopped shallots. Fry for a few minutes, then gradually pour in the stock. Bring slowly to boiling point, and continue to cook gently until the stock has been absorbed by the rice. Season with salt and pepper to taste. Stir in most of the grated cheese, the chopped raisins and the tomato sauce. Cook again for a minute or two. Arrange the savoury rice in an entrée dish and keep hot. Carefully poach the eggs in boiling water to which the lemon juice has been added. Take up, drain well and arrange on the rice: sprinkle with the remainder of the grated cheese and a pinch of paprika, finishing off with the chopped parsley. *From Miss Hannah Morgan, Herefordshire.*

CASSEROLE OF CARROTS

PUT the raw carrots through a mincer (coarsest cutter), then into a casserole with a little pepper and salt, 3 or 4 small knobs of butter and 2 tablespoonfuls of hot water. Cover and put into the oven.

Carrots take less time to cook this way, are ready chopped to serve, and all the flavour is in the vegetable and not lost in the water. *From Mrs. A. C. Thomas, Montgomeryshire.*

Two Welsh Recipes from the Hungry 'Forties

SIOT

½ cupful oat bread.   1 pint buttermilk.

CRUSH the bread (made of equal parts oatmeal and flour), and put into a basin. Pour in the buttermilk, and let the bread soak for 1 hour: when it will be ready to serve with bread and butter.

BRYWES

2 tablespoonfuls breadcrumbs.   Salt and pepper to taste.
1 tablespoonful crushed oatmeal.   ½ pint boiling water.
1 teaspoonful butter or dripping.

PUT the breadcrumbs and oatmeal into a basin, add salt and pepper to flavour, break in the dripping or butter. Pour the boiling water over it, and stand for 5 minutes before serving.

From Mrs. Williams, Caernarvonshire.

A MALTESE CABBAGE RECIPE

BARELY cover the bottom of a saucepan with lard (or dripping). In this fry 1 small clove of garlic till brown. Having washed and soaked the cabbage in the usual way, chop it finely as for pickling, and add to fat in saucepan. Add enough water to prevent burning and a pinch of salt. Cook for 10 minutes. Cabbage cooked this way is delicious. " Bubble and Squeak " is also much improved by browning a clove of garlic in the fat in which it is cooked.

From Mrs. L. J. Harper, 34 Strada Sinia, Calcare, Malta.

GROATS

I HAVE never come across this recipe anywhere but in one part of Herefordshire ; nor have I read it anywhere. But all the members of my family had the recipe and used it.

Soak the groats for at least 12 hours in water. To 2 lbs.

groats add about ¼ lb. fat cut up fine (we used to put the fat left after straining lard as well, as it may need a little extra fat.) Chop heads of leeks, or onions, and a little origany (origany was the word always used, but is better known as marjoram), pepper and salt. Boil all together till quite tender and the mixture is getting stiff. Stir frequently, as it will be apt to burn.

If it is intended to put this in skins, a little milk must be added to moisten it, but not if it is intended to fry it in pieces. A little cooked rice and chopped thyme are good added, and stirred well in. If they are put in skins, and are floured, they will keep some time.

From Miss M. Joan Parry, The White House, Ibstone, Bucks.

YORKSHIRE OLD WIVES' SOD

5 good-sized eggs.
3 gills new milk.
Pepper and salt.

Butter.
2 thin oatcakes.

BREAK the eggs into a basin and beat for 2 minutes. Add the milk and seasoning, mixing well. Have ready a baking-pan nicely greased with fresh butter. Pour in the beaten eggs and milk mixture. Next break the oatcakes into pieces about ½ in. square. Sprinkle them on top of the sod. Add a few nuts of butter and place in a moderate oven. Bake for 20 minutes. If the oatcakes are lightly toasted and buttered before breaking up they make the sod a tastier dish.

From the late Mrs. Ellen Cowking, Lancashire.

SURPRISE LOAF

Young vegetables.
A sandwich loaf.
Butter.

Lemon.
Eggs.

THIS may be made with fresh or tinned vegetables according to the season.

Chop up as many young vegetables as you want. If fresh, fry them lightly in butter, frying potatoes separately and other vegetables together according to the time that each takes to cook. Take a small sandwich loaf and scoop out the crumb, keeping the top crust for a lid. Fill the hollow loaf with the fried vegetables (or with tinned ones, strained from their liquor), and over them pour the following sauce:

Melt 2 ozs. butter and stir in 1 tablespoonful of flour; when smooth add about 1 gill milk and stir over gentle heat for

15 minutes. Beat the yolk of 1 egg into a tea-cup of cold milk and stir it into the sauce without letting it boil.

Pour it into the loaf over the vegetables, adding a squeeze of lemon. Put on the crust lid, butter it lightly, and bake in a moderate oven for about 20 minutes.

From Miss E. M. Dyer, Oxenhall, Newent, Gloucester.

VEGETABLE HOT-POT

VEGETABLES such as carrots, swede turnips, sliced parsnips, the white part of leeks, Jerusalem artichokes and onions make a very tasty hot-pot. Fry the vegetables lightly in good fat and put them into a deep stone pot of any kind. Season well with pepper and salt, especially pepper. Mix a little flour smoothly with enough water just to moisten the vegetables, pour the mixture in, put on the lid and cook slowly either in the oven or on the side of the stove for 2 hours.

From Mrs. E. G. Thomas, Pembrokeshire.

MACARONI, CURRIED

½ lb. macaroni.	1 tablespoonful curry powder.
2 onions.	2 tablespoonfuls sugar.
1 apple (sliced).	1 tablespoonful vinegar.
1 oz. margarine.	2 pints boiling water.

MAKE the margarine hot in a pan, put in sliced onions and apple, and fry for 5 minutes. Add the curry powder mixed with vinegar and sugar. Bring to the boil, then pour in boiling water and a pinch of salt. Put in the macaroni, broken into small pieces. Cook for ½ hour, and serve very hot. Slices of hard-boiled eggs make a tasty addition to this dish.

From Miss Louie Fitzpatrick, Co. Down.

SAGE AND ONION PUDDING

6 ozs. breadcrumbs.	1 teaspoonful sage.
2 ozs. oatmeal.	Seasoning.
2 tablespoonfuls chopped onion.	Milk to mix.
2 ozs. chopped suet.	

MIX all the ingredients together ; add sufficient milk to form a soft mixture. Turn into a greased tin and bake in a moderate oven about 1 hour. Cut into squares and serve with roast pork, mutton or rabbit : or it is excellent without meat if a thick brown gravy is served with it.

From Mrs. W. Bratt, Windy Bank, Somersal, Derby.

VEGETABLE MARROW STEW

1 fair-sized marrow.	A goodly-sized lump of butter.
6 medium-sized tomatoes.	1 teaspoonful Demerara sugar.
2 onions.	Salt and pepper to taste.

PEEL and remove seeds from marrow ; cut into small cubes. Skin tomatoes, peel and cut up onions. Put these together in an enamel saucepan with enough water to cover the bottom of the saucepan (no more, as the marrow will provide enough moisture). Add butter, sugar, salt and pepper to taste. Stew slowly for $1\frac{1}{2}$ to 2 hours. Serve with toast or brown bread and butter. And here you will have a meal fit for the most fastidious.

From Mrs. Gravett, Sussex.

FRIED MARROW WITH POACHED EGGS

CUT a marrow into slices, about $\frac{1}{2}$ in. thick. Pare off the rind and remove the seeds, etc. Flour each slice and brush over lightly with beaten egg. Dip into breadcrumbs, and fry in hot fat until a golden brown. Keep hot while the eggs are poached. Allow 3 or 4 slices of marrow to each egg.

The marrow slices may be dipped into batter instead ; or can be fried as they are to serve with fried rashers.

From Miss Ruth Jones, Rooks Grove Farm, Warnford, Southampton.

SAVOURY CUCUMBER

1 cucumber.	Pepper and salt.
Small piece of butter.	Dash of cayenne.
1 tablespoonful cream or top milk.	Some slices of fried bread.

PEEL the cucumber and cut into 2-in. lengths. Throw into boiling salted water, and cook until soft enough to break up. Drain well, and put in a bowl ; mash with butter, pepper and cream ; dust with a little flour. Then put into small saucepan, and simmer for a few minutes. Serve on slices of fried bread, with a little minced parsley on top.

From Miss D. Hemus, Arundel Farm, Wickenford, near Worcester.

MASHED CHESTNUTS

1 lb. of chestnuts.	Milk.
2 ozs. butter.	Pepper and salt.
3 ozs. breadcrumbs.	

TO shell the chestnuts, put them into a saucepan, with just enough water to cover them ; having first made a cut in the skin of each. Bring to the boil, cook for 2 minutes, remove from the stove, and you will find that the outer shell and inner skin will come off quite easily. After skinning, put them into another saucepan, with enough milk to cover them. Simmer gently until quite tender, then rub through a sieve, or mash until quite smooth. Return to the saucepan, add the butter and breadcrumbs, and season with pepper and salt. Stir well and serve hot.

From Mrs. F. L. Saunders, Letcombe Bassett, Berks.

CREAMED CELERY

Good head of celery.
1 pint milk.
Level teaspoonful salt.
Breadcrumbs.

1 oz. butter.
1 oz. flour.
4 ozs. finely-grated cheese.
Pepper.

WASH and clean the celery, and cut into dice enough to fill a pint measure. Put in a saucepan with the milk and salt. Cook gently till tender, then drain off the milk. In another saucepan melt the butter and mix in the flour. When quite smooth gradually add the milk in which the celery has been cooked, keeping well-stirred until it boils. It should then be thick and smooth. Let it boil for a few minutes, then add the grated cheese, a dash of pepper, and the cooked celery. Bring to the boil again, and serve with buttered breadcrumbs, *i.e.*—breadcrumbs fried in butter until a golden brown.

From Mrs. Webb, Oxfordshire.

" BOXSTY "

THIS is a dish that I have enjoyed during holidays in the West of Ireland. It has a name which I do not know how to spell, but it sounds like " Boxsty."

Peel and wash large potatoes, grate them into a basin, drain them lightly; and to each cupful of grated potatoes add 1 level teaspoonful of salt, $\frac{1}{2}$ cupful flour and enough milk to make a fairly stiff batter. Leave to stand for 1 hour, then fry like pancakes in bacon dripping. Serve hot with butter.

For boiled " Boxsty " prepare the grated potatoes in the same way, but then strain them tightly through muslin. Mix each cupful with $\frac{1}{2}$ cup of flour and 1 level teaspoonful of salt. Mix to a dough with milk, place in a floured cloth and boil the dumplings rapidly for $1\frac{1}{2}$ to 2 hours. Serve hot with butter or cut up cold and fry with bacon.

From Mrs. K. Martlew, Gathurst Hall Farm, Gathurst, Wigan.

ONION TOAST

Spanish onions.
Hot buttered toast.
Salt and pepper.

Cheese.
Mustard.

FRY some sliced Spanish onions a nice brown and spread thickly over rounds of hot buttered toast. Season. Cover with thin slices of cheese spread with a little mustard. Put into a hot oven or before a fire until the cheese is melted. Serve at once.

From Mrs. T. Cole, Hampshire.

STELK

(*An Irish recipe*)

2 doz. of the later spring onions. Those which are almost too coarse to use otherwise are best for this dish.

Potatoes.
Milk.

CHOP the onions into small lengths and simmer in milk until tender. Meanwhile, boil or steam a good dish of potatoes. When cooked, mash them with a little milk. Strain the onions and add these to the potatoes, mixing well. Serve very hot.

The correct Irish way is to add a large piece of fresh butter to each plate of stelk after serving. This makes a delicious and warming supper dish for the cool evenings. Chives may be used in place of spring onions if preferred, and make an equally appetising dish.

From Mrs. M. Cheshire, Gloucestershire.

OATMEAL AND HERB " SAUSAGES "

¾ pint salted water.
1 cupful flaked oatmeal.
1 medium-sized onion, chopped finely.
1 teaspoonful mixed herbs.
Some chopped parsley.

Salt and pepper to taste.
A little tomato sauce, if liked.
1 egg.
Some breadcrumbs.

BRING the water to the boil, stir in the oatmeal, and cook for ½ hour, stirring frequently. Pour the oatmeal mixture over the onion, herbs, parsley, salt and pepper and tomato sauce. Then add a well-beaten egg and enough fine breadcrumbs to make a stiff dough, flour the hands and roll the mixture into sausage shapes. Dip the " sausages " into flour, egg and breadcrumbs, and fry a golden brown. Serve with hot sauce.

From Mrs. V. Cantwell, Hampshire.

LEEK PIE

THIS is one of the most appetising and nourishing ways of serving one of the best of vegetables.

Take 2 lbs. of leeks, clean them and cut into lengths about $\frac{1}{2}$ in. ; put in saucepan and boil until tender, then strain and put in pie-dish, adding 2 ozs. of streaked bacon cut finely, $\frac{1}{4}$ lb. cream, 2 eggs well beaten, pepper and salt to taste. Cover with a good pastry and bake in the oven for $\frac{1}{2}$ hour. This would be sufficient for 4 persons ; more cream may be added, when serving, if available.

From Mrs. C. Tremayne, Viles Park, Buslawn, Wadebridge.

A DELICIOUS WAY OF COOKING LEEKS

Leeks.	Seasoning to taste.
Milk.	A little cream or an egg-yolk, if
Butter.	liked.
Flour.	Small rashers of bacon.

SCALD the leeks for a few minutes in boiling water and then stew them slowly in milk. Drain when tender, and make a sauce with a little butter and flour and the milk in which the leeks were cooked. A little cream or an egg-yolk may be added to the sauce if stirred in after removing from the stove. Before serving, pour the sauce over the leeks and decorate the top with tiny rolled rashers of bacon, crisply grilled.

From Miss K. L. Siddall, Yorkshire.

VEGETABLE ROLY-POLY

3 carrots.	3 potatoes (sliced).
3 parsnips.	3 tomatoes.
1 small turnip.	A little gravy powder.
Pepper and salt to taste.	Suet crust.

ROLL out the suet crust fairly thinly, sprinkle over with gravy powder. Over the crust lay the grated carrots, parsnips, turnip and sliced potatoes. Cover with a layer of sliced tomatoes, then pepper and salt to taste. Roll up in a cloth, and boil for $2\frac{1}{2}$ hours. Serve steaming hot with a little good gravy.

From Miss E. J. Watson, Somersetshire.

CHAMP

OLD potatoes, when cooked this way, are beautifully white and floury—much nicer even than new potatoes similarly treated until the latter have really come into season.

Pick as large potatoes as possible and wash thoroughly. Peel and place in a vessel containing cold water, to prevent potatoes changing colour until enough are peeled. Then boil in the usual way. Get ready a generous handful of chives, cut short with a pair of scissors ; add salt, as required, also sweet milk, but not enough to make the champ sloppy. When the potatoes are sufficiently tender, drain, set the pot firmly on the ground, and pound thoroughly with a beetle, after adding the chives and salt. Heat the milk to boiling point, pour over all, and stir well.

The usual way of serving is to lift each helping on to a plate, make a well in the centre, and quickly add a chunk of butter. Then lift each spoonful round the outer edge of the champ, dip it in the melted butter to eat.

From Miss Mary Stevenson, Bellevue, Aughnahoory, Kilkeel, Co. Down.

POTATO OMELETTES

3 cupfuls mashed potatoes.   ½ cupful hot milk.
½ teaspoonful salt.   ½ teaspoonful pepper.
1 egg.

MIX all the ingredients together, and season to taste. Cook a tablespoonful at a time on a hot, greased girdle, or in a small frying-pan ; turn each omelette when brown, and brown also on the other side. Serve with grilled chops.

POTATO AND CHEESE SAUCE

4 to 6 cooked potatoes.   1 oz. butter : ½ pint milk.
3 ozs. grated cheese.   1 tablespoonful breadcrumbs.

CUT the potatoes into slices. Melt the butter in a saucepan, add the milk and bring slowly to the boil. Add 2 ozs. of the cheese ; simmer for a few minutes. Arrange the sliced potatoes in a pie-dish ; pour over the sauce ; mix the breadcrumbs and the remaining 1 oz. of cheese together. Sprinkle over top of pie, and brown in the oven.

BAKED CHEESE POTATOES

6 baked potatoes.   1 gill hot milk.
A little salt.   1½ tablespoonfuls butter.
¾ cupful grated cheese.

WHEN the potatoes are cooked, cut them in halves lengthwise. Scoop out the inside, and mash it. Mix in the butter, salt, cheese, milk and a little pepper. Pile this mixture into the shells. Sprinkle with cheese. Put in a greased dish, and bake in a moderate oven until crisp and brown on top.

These three recipes are all from Mrs. Skelton, Tallantire.

STUFFED MARROW RINGS

YOU will need marrow, tomatoes, bacon, breadcrumbs, egg, seasoning and chopped mint.

First prepare your baking-dish. Cover the bottom with lukewarm water, to which add 2 tablespoons of liquid dripping : then stir in 1 heaped tablespoonful of seasoned flour (pepper and salt seasoning) previously mixed into a paste with water. Stir all together and keep warm whilst preparing the marrow.

Peel and core the marrow, cut into rings about 1 in. thick (allowing 1 ring per person), lay in the baking-pan. Next take tomatoes (large enough for one to go inside the marrow ring). Cut the top off each and scoop out the inside, mix in a basin with 2 ozs. of breadcrumbs, pepper, salt and a little mustard, pour over 1 gill of boiling milk, add 2 rashers of chopped bacon (lean preferred), and beat together with a small egg. Fill the tomato cases with this mixture, give a good sprinkling of finely-chopped mint, and put inside the marrow rings.

Dot the marrow rings with knobs of dripping, cover with greaseproof and bake in a moderate oven for about 40 minutes. After 20 minutes take away greaseproof and baste the marrow rings. Serve with brown gravy made from stock in the baking-tin.

If the marrow is old, bake it about 20 minutes before putting the tomatoes in and have an extra cup of water in the baking-tin.

From Mrs. F. A. Foden, The Scarr, Newent, Glos.

CORNISH POTATO CAKE

½ lb. boiled potato.
½ oz. butter.

2 ozs. flour.
A pinch of salt.

MASH the boiled potatoes, while hot, with the butter, and mix well together ; add salt, sprinkle in flour, mix evenly. Roll out very thin on a floured board. Cut out in rounds about the size of a saucer, and place on a hot girdle or greased frying-pan ; prick with a fork and cook 3 minutes on each side. Serve hot. *From Miss B. Olver, Woodland Valley Farm, Ladock, Cornwall.*

ONION CAKE

HAVE ready a nice bright cake-tin and butter it well. Peel some potatoes and slice them, laying them at the bottom of the tin. On this sprinkle some finely-chopped onion and some tiny bits of butter. Sprinkle with pepper and salt. Repeat these layers until the cake-tin is full, pressing each potato layer firmly down, and a potato layer with bits of butter on it must be the last. Cover with a plate and bake in a moderate oven for 1 hour. This is delicious with hot or cold meat.

From Mrs. Rogers, Acton Park, Wrexham.

POTATO PASTIES

½ lb. mashed potatoes, cold.
2 teaspoonfuls baking powder.
6 ozs. butter.

Tomato sauce.
A little cooked meat.
½ lb. flour.

SIFT the flour, rub in the butter. Add the baking powder and stir in the sieved potatoes with cold water to make stiff dough. Roll out and cut in suitable lengths. Set out seasoned meat, slightly moistened with tomato sauce, on one half. Fold other half over. Press edges together, prick and bake light brown. *From Mrs. J. R. Robinson, Long Sowerby, Carlisle, Cumberland.*

POTATO AND CHEESE SAVOURY

HERE is a recipe which our family is very fond of. It is cheap and nourishing and very appetising.

For 6 people you will require : 3 lbs. potatoes, 1 pint milk, 1 oz. butter, salt, pepper and grated nutmeg to taste and chopped parsley, 3 ozs. grated cheese. Boil the milk with seasoning and butter and cut the peeled potatoes in ⅛ in. slices. Place in a pan and pour the boiling milk over and let cook very slowly for 1 hour ; just before serving add the grated cheese and parsley. *From Mrs. E. Gordon, Welshpool, Montgomeryshire.*

FLAKED RICE CHEESE PUDDING

1 cup shredded cheese.
1 cup flaked rice.
1 cup breadcrumbs.

1 small onion chopped finely.
Pepper and salt.
2 ozs. butter.

MIX well with milk to the thickness of batter, and turn into a greased pudding-basin. Steam or boil for ¾ hour and serve hot. This is a savoury pudding easily made and quickly cooked and makes a light tasty dish for invalids.

From Mrs. W. Wagstaff, Norwell, near Newark, Notts.

CHEESE AND TOMATO PIE

WELL grease a pie-dish and put in it a thick layer of stale breadcrumbs (which have previously been soaked in milk to a pulp), then a layer of grated cheese with a little grated suet : then a good, thick layer of sliced tomatoes (or just halved tomatoes), pepper and salt, and a few little knobs of butter on the tomatoes. Add another layer of the soaked breadcrumbs. Cover with a little batter and bake in a moderate oven. Serve hot.   *From Miss B. Higgs, Stony Stratford, Bucks.*

CHEESE SAVOURY

1 lb. onions.   3 ozs. cheese.
¼ lb. spaghetti.   1½ ozs. butter.

BOIL onions, then chop into slices. Put spaghetti into salted water and cook until soft, and grate cheese. Butter a pie-dish, put a layer of spaghetti, then onions, then cheese. Season to taste. Add alternately until dish is full. Sprinkle a little cheese on top, dot with lumps of butter and bake in moderate oven until nicely browned.

From Miss W. L. Wedd, Bassingbourn, near Royston, Herts.

A SAVOURY FROM BREAD SAUCE

IF by any chance you have some bread sauce left over, try using it up like this. Put it into a basin, add a very little milk, if necessary, and some grated cheese. Mix well, put into buttered cocotte dishes, scatter a very little grated cheese on top and put a tiny piece of butter on each, bake in a moderate oven till brown.

From Mrs. H. Handy, Arthingworth Lodge, Market Harborough, Leics.

COTSWOLD DUMPLINGS

2 whole eggs.   4 ozs. grated cheese.
2 ozs. butter.

STIR grated cheese and creamed butter together, add beaten egg and pepper and salt to taste, and enough white bread-crumbs to make into a stiff mixture. Form into dumplings, roll in breadcrumbs and fry in hot fat a biscuit brown. Serve with vegetable purée, preferably tomato, broccoli or onion.

From Miss K. M. Chappell, Sawcombe Farm, Ozleworth, Glos.

COTTAGE CHEESE

PLACE a jugful of sour milk in a warm place until the milk is quite thick, then salt should be added in the porportion of ½ small teaspoonful to a pint. Stir well, and place in a muslin bag. (Well-washed flour bags do excellently for the purpose.) Hang it up to drain overnight, press between two plates for an hour, then work up with fresh cream and make into a pat.

From Mrs. Robert Thomson, Dumfriesshire.

APPLE MARIGOLD

3 large cooking apples.
2 eggs.
1 teacupful milk.
1 teaspoonful marigold petals.
· 1 teaspoonful sweet thyme.

1 teaspoonful sage.
1 small pepper corn crushed
    to powder.
Butter.

PEEL and core the apples and cut in rings. Beat the eggs in
    the milk, season with the marigold, thyme, sage and pepper-
corn. Put mixture in a shallow dish, carefully place apple rings
on top with 1 or 2 pieces of butter. Bake in a good oven from
20 to 25 minutes. *From Mrs. J. Preston, Oxfordshire.*

CAROLINA CARROTS

8 medium-sized carrots.
¾ breakfastcupful grated cheese.
½ breakfastcupful brown bread-
    crumbs.
2 large-sized tomatoes.

1 tablespoonful salt.
A pinch of pepper.
1½ teacupfuls cooked rice.
Margarine.

SCRAPE the carrots and cook in boiling salted water till
    tender. Hollow out one side of carrots, and remove a
thin slice from the other side ; so that they will lie flat in a tin.
Add cheese, crumbs, tomato, milk and seasoning to the rice.
Stuff the carrots with the mixture and place in a greased baking-
tin. Place a few dabs of margarine on top, and bake in a hot
oven for about 20 minutes.

From Mrs. H. Betteridge, Old Lowe, Much Dewchurch, Hereford.

TURNIP AU GRATIN

1 turnip.
2 tablespoonfuls grated cheese.
1 teacupful breadcrumbs.

1 small teacupful milk.
2 tablespoonfuls cream.
Margarine.

PEEL the turnip and cut into squares. Put in salted water and
    parboil for 10 minutes. Strain and cut the turnip into slices.
Put into a greased pie-dish, season to taste, dot with pieces of
margarine. Pour over the milk and cream, cover with breadcrumbs, sprinkle the cheese over all. Bake for ½ an hour in
a hot oven. *From Mrs. Kemp, Mayfield, St. Ola, Kirkwall, Orkney.*

TURNIP PIE

(Here is an unusual and delicious way of serving turnips)

WASH 4 new turnips, and put into plenty of boiling water
    slightly salted. Allow to boil for about ½ hour, or till
they are almost cooked. Take them out of the water, peel

and cut them into thin slices. Put into a pie-dish, and sprinkle a little salt and pepper over them. Add a teacupful of milk, and cover with breadcrumbs and a little grated cheese. Put the dish in an oven or in front of the fire until nicely browned on top.

Anon.

MUSHROOM PANCAKES

Batter :

½ lb. flour.
½ pint milk.
2 tablespoonfuls water.
2 ozs. grated cheese.

2 eggs.
A little salt and pepper to taste.
Lard for frying.

Filling :

½ lb. peeled and chopped mushrooms.
2 ozs. grated cheese.
1 small finely-grated onion.

1 teaspoonful chopped parsley.
1 egg.
Butter for frying.

MAKE a batter with the flour, eggs, milk and water; and beat until smooth. Leave for an hour. Then add the cheese, and season to taste with salt and pepper. Put a little lard into the frying-pan; when smoking hot, pour in a little of the batter. Cook on both sides till brown, then spread with a thick layer of the filling. To make the filling, mix the mushrooms, cheese, onion and parsley together; season and fry in the butter. When sufficiently cooked, stir in the beaten egg to bind the mixture. Roll up and serve hot. This quantity is sufficient for 6 pancakes.

From Mrs. E. Cruse, Worcestershire.

COD'S ROE PASTE

SCRAPE all the cooked cod's roe away from the skin, add to taste pepper, salt, mustard (made with vinegar) and a little butter, then beat all well together and pound into a smooth paste. Press it into small basins or glass jars and allow to get cold, then pour over the top some oiled butter, which when set will form a protective covering and the paste will keep for several weeks. This paste can be used as a sandwich filling or as a savoury piled on hot buttered toast, or on bread and butter or toast at tea-time.

From Miss I. Turner, Easton Farm, Pylle, Shepton Mallet, Somerset.

PUDDINGS

ECONOMY BREAD PUDDING

1 lb. soaked bread.	4 ozs. margarine.
6 ozs. self-raising flour.	½ teacupful milk.
6 ozs. moist sugar.	1 dessertspoonful vinegar.
2 tablespoonsful marmalade.	

FOR this you can use your stale crusts or pieces of dry bread, and the quantity given here is ample for 4 or 5 persons. The bread must, of course, be well soaked in water, and also well squeezed out of the water. Beat the margarine and sugar together, then add the bread and flour. When it is well mixed, add the milk; to which the vinegar has been added. Beat well and put in a basin that has been well greased and lined with the marmalade. Cover with greaseproof paper and a cloth, plunge into boiling water, and boil steadily for 2 hours.

If preferred, jam may be used in place of marmalade; or 6 ozs. of fruit added to the mixture makes a delightful change. Again, chopped dates could be added in place of either; so it is really a recipe from which you can make three different puddings.

From Mrs. I. Goldsmith, Lands Farm Cottage, Willingdon, Eastbourne,
Sussex.

BREAD AND MIXED FRUIT PUDDING

STALE bread, of course, need never be wasted; there are endless ways in which it can be used up. One of the best ways is in a bread pudding, and here is a recipe I can recommend.

Cut some bread into neat dice, put them in a greased pie-dish, and pour sufficient milk over just to cover. Leave till soft, then add more cold milk, to which has been added 1 or 2 eggs according to the size of the pudding; some sultanas, currants, raisins or stoned dates and sugar to taste. Stir the mixture very carefully with a fork, being careful not to break the dice: put a few pieces of butter here and there and bake in a moderate oven until a golden brown.

Mrs. H. Handy, Arthingworth Lodge, Market Harborough, Leics.

" BREAD BETTY "

SOMETIMES I have toast left over as well as bread and butter, and this is how I use it up :

Butter the toast and cut it into dice, enough to fill 4 cupfuls. Mix it with ½ cupful of grated or chopped walnuts and 2 cupfuls of raisins previously soaked in orange juice. Arrange this mixture in a well-buttered pie-dish and sprinkle a little brown sugar among the layers.

Have ready a few slices of buttered bread, which should be put on top as a lid, buttered side on top. Pour over all ½ pint of milk, in which you have beaten an egg and a teaspoonful of honey, and sprinkle a little nutmeg on top. Bake as you would an ordinary egg custard in not too hot an oven.

Mrs. Constance Berry, Kimberley House, Leire, Rugby.

GOOSEBERRY BREAD PUDDING

1 pint young gooseberries.
1 thick slice of white bread.

1½ gills milk.
2 eggs.

CUT the crust off the bread, on to which pour the boiling milk. Cover this with a plate and let it stand for ½ hour, then crush the bread and beat in the eggs. Add 1 pint of young gooseberries which have previously been topped, tailed and washed. Mix well together, put into a well-greased basin and cover with greased paper. Steam for 1 hour. Do not add sugar before cooking.

From Mrs. W. Evans, Wellington, Salop.

TREACLE SPONGE

6 ozs. flour.
A good teaspoonful baking powder (or, if a very dark sponge is preferred, use bi-carbonate of soda, mixed smooth in a spoonful of milk).

4 ozs. suet.
Grated rind of 1 lemon.
1 egg.
1 wineglassful milk.
6 ozs. golden syrup.

MIX the flour and suet together, add lemon rind, beaten egg, bi-carbonate of soda (if used), milk and syrup. Put in a greased basin with 2 pieces of greaseproof paper tied very securely over the top. Place basin in a saucepan with boiling water to come half-way up, and steam for 3 hours. Serve with hot custard.

(The best way to measure syrup is to scatter plenty of flour on the scales, and pour syrup on the flour. It will be found to come away all together.) *From Miss M. I. Owen, Nottinghamshire.*

OATMEAL PUDDING

½ lb. plain flour.
½ lb. fine oatmeal.
1½ teaspoonfuls ground ginger.
1 egg.
Little milk for mixing.

1 teaspoonful baking powder.
¼ lb. sugar.
3 tablespoonfuls golden syrup.
½ lb. shredded suet.

MIX dry ingredients together, add beaten egg to the warmed golden syrup, and stir into the dry ingredients. Mix to about the consistency of a cake, adding as much milk as required. Put into a greased pie-dish, and bake in a moderate oven for about 1½ hours. Turn out on to a hot dish, and serve with hot golden syrup. *From Miss L. Stean, Cheshire.*

EMERGENCY FRUIT PUDDING

1 lb. seedless raisins.
1 lb. currants.
1 lb. stoned dates.
½ lb. chopped mixed peel.
1 lb. sugar.
1 lb. suet.
½ oz. mixed spice.

¾ lb. flour.
¼ lb. breadcrumbs.
1 lb. each of grated apples and carrots.
3 eggs.
The juice of a lemon.
A little milk.

MIX together dry ingredients, beat up the eggs with a little milk, add the juice of a lemon and blend thoroughly with the other ingredients. Prepare some stone jam-jars; fill with the mixture, cover with greased paper and boil for 4 hours. When cool store on a shelf where they will keep for weeks ready for use.

When required stand the jar in a saucepan of boiling water to re-heat; and in the same pan stand another jar of milk which can be sweetened and thickened with eggs to make a sauce for the pudding. *From Miss Joyce Francis, Alconbury House Farm, Huntingdon.*

RHUBARB SPONGE

1 large cupful cooked rhubarb (cold).
2 ozs. butter.
1 large cupful flour.

1 egg.
2 ozs. sugar.
½ teaspoonful baking powder.
¼ teaspoonful salt.

GREASE a pie-dish well, pour in the stewed rhubarb. Beat the butter and sugar until creamy, add the egg, salt and baking powder, then sift in the flour gradually, stirring all together until the mixture is well blended. If it is rather thick, a little milk should be added. Spread the mixture evenly over the rhubarb, and cook in a hot oven for 20 minutes. Serve hot or cold with custard.

From Miss M. Broad, Castletown, Faindon, near Chester.

FIG PUDDING

5 ozs. flour.
2½ ozs. grated suet.
¼ lb. chopped figs.
¾ gill syrup.
¾ gill sour milk.

1 egg.
¼ teaspoonful grated nutmeg.
½ teaspoonful cinnamon.
½ teaspoonful ginger.
½ teaspoonful bi-carbonate of soda.

MIX the dry ingredients, suet and figs together, add the warmed syrup, beaten egg and milk. Pour into a greased basin and steam for 2 hours. Serve with sugar and cream.

From Miss M. C. Utley, Watchet, Somerset.

YORKSHIRE APPLE PUDDING

½ lb. self-raising flour.
2 eggs.
1 pint milk.

A good pinch of salt.
2 large baking apples.
Dripping.

SIFT flour and salt into a basin, break in the eggs and add half the milk. Stir with a wooden spoon to a smooth paste and beat well. Then add the rest of the milk a little at a time. See that the mixture is free from lumps. Peel 2 large baking apples and grate them into the mixture, stirring well. Melt about 2 ozs. dripping in a Yorkshire pudding-tin until very hot; then pour in the batter at once and bake in a hot oven for about 40 minutes. Serve dredged well with sugar.

From Miss Sumnel, Primrose Hill Farm, Darnhall, Winsford, Cheshire.

LEMON CURD SPONGE PUDDING

4 ozs. margarine or butter.
4 ozs. sugar.
4 ozs. flour.
2 eggs.
½ teaspoonful baking powder.

1 oz. currants.
Lemon curd.
A pinch of salt.
A little milk.

BEAT butter and sugar to a cream, add well-beaten eggs, sift in flour by degrees, stirring all the time; add about 2 tablespoonfuls of milk and beat well. Put about two-thirds of the mixture in a well-greased pie-dish, then a layer of lemon curd, sprinkle currants over the lemon curd, then the remainder of the mixture. Bake in a moderate oven for about 40 minutes. For 5 or 6 people. *From Mrs. M. I. Bell, Poolharn Hall, Horncastle, Lincs.*

PEAR AND GINGER PUDDING

BUTTER a pudding-basin and coat with breadcrumbs. Mix 4 ozs. breadcrumbs with 2 ozs. grated suet. Prepare 1 lb. pears and grate them with the rind of a lemon, adding sugar to taste, and 1 oz. chopped preserved ginger. Put a third of the bread mixture into the basin ; then half of the pears ; another third of the bread ; then the remainder of the pears ; and cover with the rest of the bread mixture. Cover with greased paper and steam for 2 hours. Serve with sweet white sauce. This has a delicious flavour.

From Mrs. W. Symes, Farnham Moor, Sharperton, Morpeth,
Northumberland.

JANE'S CHOCOLATE SPONGE

7 ozs. self-raising flour.	2 eggs.
1 small teaspoonful salt.	1 large tablespoonful of coffee
3 ozs. chocolate.	essence.
5 ozs. butter.	A few drops of vanilla essence.

SLIGHTLY warm butter, add sugar, beat until creamy. Beat yolks of eggs well, and add to butter and sugar. Mix chocolate powder, salt and flour together, stir into the mixture. Add coffee essence in a tablespoonful of warm milk. Beat the whites of eggs to a stiff froth, add vanilla essence and fold into the mixture gently. Add 1 teaspoonful of boiling water just before putting mixture into well-papered tin. Bake in fairly sharp oven for 1 to 1½ hours.

Care must be taken not to have the milk too warm.

Mrs. D. L. Brown, Overhall, Colne Engaine, Earls Colne, Essex.

LITTLE BILLINGHAM PUDDING

6 ozs. self-raising flour.	6 ozs. chopped stoned dates.
A pinch of salt.	4 ozs. shredded suet.
2 ozs. white breadcrumbs.	2 ozs. seedless raisins.
Milk (less than ½ pint).	2 tablespoonfuls liquid honey.

MIX together all the dry ingredients. Then add sufficient milk to make into a stiff dough, and finally stir in the honey. Put the mixture into a well-greased basin, allowing room to rise. Cover with 2 thicknesses of greaseproof paper and steam for 2½ to 3 hours. Turn out and serve hot with whipped cream, sweet sauce or hard sauce as desired.

From Mrs. M. B. N. Allender, West Billingham Farm, Chillerton,
Newport, I.O.W.

BLANCMANGE VARIATIONS

FOLLOW the usual routine for making the ordinary cornflour pudding with 1 pint of milk and a little extra sugar to 2½ tablespoonfuls cornflour.

(1) With a little cold milk, mix into a smooth paste 2 tablespoonfuls of ground almonds and 1 heaped tablespoonful of

chocolate powder. Add this paste gradually to the cornflour pudding while still very hot, and mix thoroughly. The result makes an appetising and nourishing sweet, which is equally palatable, either cold or hot. If cold it looks most attractive in individual dishes garnished with whipped cream, whole blanched almonds, glacé cherries or angelica.

(2) Desiccated coco-nut may be substituted for ground almonds, in which case it is better to cook the coco-nut in the pudding to bring out the flavour.

(3) Coffee flavouring may be preferred to either of the chocolate-nut combinations. In this case, care must be taken that the milk pudding is definitely well below boiling point before adding coffee essence, or the milk may curdle.

From Mrs. Mary Cowles, Post Office Farm, Stutton, near Ipswich, Suffolk.

GOOSEBERRY PUDDING

1 quart green gooseberries.
¼ lb. sugar.
2 eggs.
1 oz. butter.
¼ lb. breadcrumbs.

STEW the fruit gently till it will pulp, then beat it up. Take 1 pint of this pulp, add the other ingredients, mix all together, except the eggs which should not be added till the mixture is quite cool, and then stirred in thoroughly. Put the mixture into a buttered dish and bake for ½ hour. Strew a little sifted sugar over the pudding before serving.

From Mrs. E. A. Thomas, Ty-Ishaf Farm, Llanharry, Glam.

FRUMENTY AND FLUFFIN

FRUMENTY, which is an old yeoman farmer's dish, and Fluffin were made at Christmas time. The old custom was to sup a wee bowl on Christmas Eve, and offer it to the stranger within the door. It is a great favourite in the districts of Stockton-on-Tees and Coxhoe.

To make Fluffin, simmer enough barley and milk until it is as smooth as velvet. Add enough grated nutmeg and sugar to taste, and a few drops of brandy.

Frumenty takes a lot of cooking. Simmer enough kibbled wheat for 12 hours ; then add a nut of butter, mixed spice, currants (if liked), sugar, cream and rum. It is as near a liquid spice loaf as one can imagine, delightful and fragrant. One farmer I heard described it as " Gruel with its best clothes on."

Mrs. E. Symes, Farnham Tilery, Sharperton, Morpeth, Northumberland.

HATTED KIT
(*A very old Highland dish*)

WARM slightly over the fire 2 pints of buttermilk. Pour it into a dish and carry it to the side of a cow. Milk into it about 1 pint of milk, having previously put into the dish sufficient rennet for the whole.

After allowing it to stand for a while, lift the curd, place it on a sieve, and press the whey through until the curd is quite stiff. Season with sugar and nutmeg before serving. Whip some thick cream, season it also with a little grated nutmeg and sugar, and mix gently with the curd. This dish can quite well be made without milking the cow into it, although direct milking puts a better " hat " on the Kit.

From Miss H. Stuart, Cairndoon, Whithorn, Wigtonshire, Scotland.

HONEY NUT TARTLETS

6 ozs. flour.
½ cup sour cream.
Salt.
½ lb. butter (slightly salted or fresh).

1 yolk of egg.
Honey.
Walnuts.
Castor sugar (or Demerara).

SIFT the flour with a pinch of salt, rub in the butter, and blend with the beaten egg yolk and cream. Leave in a cool place for a time, then roll out and line small tartlet-tins with the paste. Mix together 1 teaspoonful of honey with 1 teaspoonful of Demerara sugar and 1 teaspoonful of minced walnuts, fill up the tartlet-tin, and bake in a moderate oven till brown and crisp.

Mrs. V. Cantwell, Rotherbank Farm, Liss, Hants.

LEMON CURD DUMPLINGS

THESE dumplings are better made in small individual moulds to prevent any water getting in to spoil lemon curd centres.

Well grease some small moulds and line with thinly-rolled suet paste made with 4 ozs. shredded suet, 8 ozs. flour, salt, and mixed with cold water. Make a curd-filling by well beating 2 eggs and adding 1 teacupful castor sugar, juice and grated rind of 1 large, or 2 small lemons, and 2 ozs. fresh melted butter. Whip all together and nearly fill each dumpling. Cover tops with a lid of paste. Squeeze the edges together well. Tie over with greased paper and steam for 1¼ hours. Turn out carefully and sift with a little fine sugar and serve hot.

From Mrs. R. Cruse, The Elms, Wadborough, Worcs.

MIXED FRUIT STIRABOUT

THIS is an old farmhouse recipe and can be used with all kinds of fresh fruit, rhubarb, gooseberries, currants, raspberries, etc., alone or mixed. Mix 4 ozs. flour with 2 ozs. butter and a pinch of salt, add 2 ozs. sugar and 2 breakfastcupfuls of picked fruit (rhubarb cut into neat cubes). Mix with milk to the consistency of a thick batter and bake in a hot oven for about 30 minutes. Serve with sugar and thick cream.

From Miss Peggy Crawford, Lowesby, Leicester.

LEMON PIE

LINE a deep plate with your favourite pastry. Make a custard by taking ¾ pint of milk and 1½ tablespoonfuls cornflour, mixed to a paste with a little of the milk. Grate the rind and juice of 2 lemons into the custard when cooled down a little, add sugar to taste. Then stir in the yolks of 2 eggs, place mixture on pastry, and bake in a nice oven. When ready, whip up the whites very stiffly, fold in 2 tablespoonfuls of castor sugar, and brown in a cool oven.

From A. E. Lamb, Derbyshire.

SNOW BALLS

PARE as many apples as you will require ; take out the cores with a small scoop ; do not break the apples. Fill the space with stoned raisins. Have some rice that has been well steeped in milk, place enough rice on a cloth to hold an apple, then draw up corners and tie round with tape or string as you would a dumpling. Set in a shallow pan with enough cold water to cover them ; bring to the boil and simmer for 1 hour. Remove them carefully without breaking, and serve with cream or melted butter.

From Mrs. Goad, Congell, Dent, Sedbergh, Yorks.

APPLE CRISPS

4 good-sized cooking apples.	1 cupful brown sugar.
½ cupful margarine.	1 cupful flour.

GREASE a baking-dish, and ¾ fill with sliced apple. Work the margarine, sugar and flour together until the mixture is like granulated sugar. Spread it over the apples. Bake in a hot oven for 10 minutes, then reduce the heat, and bake until the apples are soft and the crumbs nicely browned. Serve with cream or thin egg custard.

From Mrs. G. Rose, Broadpool Farm, Warboys Fen, Huntingdonshire.

APPLE DELIGHT

6 ozs. self-raising flour.	2 ozs. sugar.
3 ozs. lard.	1 egg white.
1 lb. cooking apples.	A pinch of salt.

MAKE a short pastry by rubbing the fat and a pinch of salt into the flour. Roll out pastry and line a sandwich-tin; bake until golden brown. Peel, core and slice the apples, cook with sugar and a little water until very soft. Beat up with a fork and fill the pastry. Whisk the egg white until stiff and spread evenly on apple. Return to the oven for a few minutes to brown and when cold decorate with a little black-currant jam. Serve cold with custard.

From Miss A. Evrall, Highfields Farm, Corley, near Coventry,
Warwickshire.

SPICE BUN

1 oz. butter.	1 teaspoonful baking powder.
4 ozs. flour.	1 egg.
2 ozs. sugar.	1 tablespoonful golden syrup.
2 ozs. currants : 1 oz. sultanas.	Short pastry.

LINE a sandwich-tin with short pastry, leaving enough pastry for cross bars. Rub butter into flour; add all dry ingredients and syrup; add the egg (well beaten) and baking powder. Turn into lined tin, put the cross bar over the top, bake ½ hour in moderate oven.

From Mrs. Steward, Siam Hall, Boxford, Colchester.

STUFFED APPLES

TAKE some large cooking apples and core them. Prick over with a fork to prevent them bursting. Next prepare the filling as follows: 2 ozs. stoned dates (chopped), 1 oz. walnuts, 1 oz. brown sugar, grated rind of 1 lemon, juice of 1 lemon. Mix all the ingredients together. Put some of the filling into the core. Put the apples in a pie-dish, with some water. Cook in a moderate oven until the apples are soft.

From Miss L. Rice, Penlan, Neath, Glam.

BANANA POPOVERS

MIX together 1 cupful flour with 1 cupful milk, 1 unbeaten egg and a pinch of salt. Stir thoroughly, using a wooden spoon. Butter some cups and place them in the oven; and when hissing hot, pour in the batter, filling each cup half full. Drop into each a piece of banana. Bake in a hot oven until puffed and golden brown, then cover with paper and finish baking.

From Miss M. Palmer, Waterloo Farm, Stow Bedon, Attleborough.

c*

LUNCHEON CAKE

1½ lbs. flour.
1 lb. sultanas.
¾ lb. butter
6 ozs. brown sugar.
1 oz. nutmeg, grated.

1 teaspoonful bi-carbonate of soda.
A pinch of salt.
1 pint buttermilk, or as much as is needed to mix to a nice consistency.

RUB the butter into the flour and mix thoroughly all the dry ingredients. Stir in the buttermilk last, with the bi-carbonate of soda dissolved in it (sour milk can be used). Bake in a slow oven for 2 hours.

From Mrs. Rose Davies, Bank House Farm, Chadwick, Bromsgrove,
Worcs.

PINEAPPLE UPSIDE-DOWN PUDDING

BUTTER a round pan about 8 in. in diameter and 3 in. deep. In it melt 1 cup brown sugar and 2 tablespoonfuls butter. On the sugar, after melting, lay as many slices of pineapple as the pan will hold. Pour over the fruit a batter of ¾ cupful milk, ½ cupful butter, ¾ cupful granulated sugar, 2 well-beaten eggs, 2 teaspoonfuls baking powder, ½ teaspoonful salt, ½ teaspoonful flavouring, 2 cupfuls flour. Beat the butter and sugar to a cream, add the eggs with a little of the flour. Sieve the dry ingredients and fold in. Bake in a moderate oven from 45 to 60 minutes. Turn at once on to a hot dish. Serve with whipped cream or custard.

From Mrs. Anderson, Guelt, Old Cumnock, Ayrshire.

POTATO CHEESE CAKES (SWEET)

¼ lb. mashed potatoes.
¼ lb. butter.
¼ lb. sugar.
2 ozs. currants.

1 egg.
A little jam.
Puff pastry.

BEAT the butter and sugar to a cream, add to the potatoes and currants; then add the egg, well beaten. Line tins with puff pastry, put in a little jam and add 1 teaspoonful of the above mixture. Bake in a quick oven until light brown.

From Mrs. J. R. Robinson, 31 Prescott Road, Long Sowerby, Carlisle.

BLACK-CURRANT LEAF CREAM

BLACK-CURRANT leaves are most delicately scented in the spring and then is the time to use them for flavouring sweets and all kinds of creams and puddings.

This is my own special recipe: Boil 1 lb. white sugar with ½ pint water and a cupful of *young* black-currant leaves. Boil, without stirring, for 15 minutes; then strain and pour the hot

74

syrup *very gently* on to 2 beaten egg whites. Beat all the time, until the mixture begins to thicken; then stir in the juice of a lemon and a gill of whipped cream.

Served in individual glasses, it is the most delicious sweet.

From Mrs. R. Johnstone, The Linkins, Castle Douglas, Kircudbright,
Scotland.

GOOSEBERRY CUSTARD CAKE

½ pint stewed, sweetened gooseberries.
2 eggs.
1 cupful castor sugar.
1¼ cupfuls self-raising flour.

The grated rind of 1 orange.
½ cupful orange juice.
1 tablespoonful lemon juice.
½ pint thick custard sauce.
⅓ cupful of margarine or vegetable
  cooking fat.

BEAT the fat to a cream in a basin. Stir in the sugar and beaten egg yolks. Beat thoroughly and then add the grated orange rind and the strained lemon juice. Sift the flour and a pinch of salt together, then add alternately with the strained orange juice. Fold in the stiffly-frothed egg-whites and bake in two deep round sandwich-tins for about 20 minutes, until firm and golden.

Remove from the oven, allow to stand for a few minutes, then turn on to a hot dish lined with a lace paper d'oyley, sprinkled with castor sugar. Put the two halves together with thick custard sauce, place the drained gooseberries on top and add more custard sauce.

From Miss E. Williams, Ty-mawr Farm, St. Brides, Wentlooge,
near Newport, Mon.

RHUBARB AND BANANA PIE

1 lb. rhubarb.
3 ozs. sugar.
The grated rind of ½ a lemon.
4 bananas.

1 egg white
2 ozs. almonds.
2 tablespoonfuls castor sugar.

WASH the rhubarb and cut into small lengths, put into a pie-dish and sprinkle with lemon rind and the sugar. Peel the bananas, crush and beat to pulp with the castor sugar; when soft beat in the white of the egg. Continue beating until quite stiff. Spread on the top of rhubarb to form a crust, sprinkle the top with blanched almonds, and bake in a moderate oven for ½ hour. Serve hot with custard or cream.

From Mrs. J. W. Foster, Westonby Lodge, Egton, Yorks.

FIG AND RAISIN PASTIES

1 lb. cooking figs.
1 lb. stoned raisins.
1 lb. Demerara sugar.

1 lemon.
1 teaspoonful ground cinnamon.
1 tablespoonful cornflour.

WASH and soak the figs until plump. Cut them in small pieces, put in saucepan with raisins, and sugar and lemon, cover with water, and stew until very tender. Mix the cornflour and cinnamon with a little water, add to the mixture, and cook for another $\frac{1}{4}$ of an hour. Then pot for use. It should be of the consistency of jam. Roll out short pastry the size of a dinner plate, spread half with some of the fig and raisin mixture, moisten edges, turn over the plain half, pinch edges and cut a row of holes down the pastry with fork or pastry scissors. Bake in a steady oven.

From Mrs. E. G. Mactier, Wigtownshire.

SPICED PLUM TART

Pastry:

8 ozs. flour.
4 ozs. butter.
$\frac{1}{4}$ teaspoonful cinnamon.

A pinch of mixed spice.
2 teaspoonfuls castor sugar.
Water.

Filling:

1 lb. plums.
4 small apples.

4 ozs. castor sugar.
2 tablespoonfuls water.

MIX all dry ingredients together to a stiff paste with cold water. Line a shallow tin with some of the paste.

Put in fruit filling. Cover with the rest of the pastry and bake $\frac{3}{4}$ hour. Remove from tin and serve hot or cold.

From Mrs. E. J. Waters, Pembrokeshire.

MARROW AND APPLE PIE

1 lb. prepared marrow.
$\frac{1}{2}$ lb. sliced apples.
Shortcrust pastry.

2 ozs. seedless raisins.
1 lemon.
Sugar.

PREPARE the marrow, and cut into small pieces. Fill a pie-dish with layers of marrow, sliced apples and raisins, sprinkling each layer with a little sugar and grated lemon-rind. Pile the mixture rather high in the centre of the dish, and add just a little water. Cover with pastry, and bake in a good oven for 1 hour or a little longer according to the apples.

Pears also can be used in this way.

From Mrs. R. Weston, Lincolnshire.

FRUIT FRUSHIE

THIS is an excellent way of using up windfalls quickly.
Take 1 lb. apples, cut up small, cook with some brown
sugar, a teaspoonful of lemon juice and a little water. When
almost done add ¼ lb. each of currants and sultanas. Stir for
2 minutes and then stand aside. Make a sweet paste with
½ lb. flour, ¼ lb. butter, 2 ozs. sugar and milk. Line a tart
plate with half the paste. Put in the fruit, then cover with the
other half. Brush with milk and bake in a hot oven 20 to 30
minutes. This is a delicious dessert dish or sliced for tea.

From Mrs. T. Waddell, Forge Farm, Bestwood, Nottingham.

OLDBURY TARTS (GLOUCESTERSHIRE)

2 lbs. flour.   ½ lb. butter.
½ lb. lard.   1 small teacupful boiling water.
Gooseberries.   Demerara sugar.

PUT the flour into the pastry bowl, and make a well in the
middle of it : into the well put the butter and lard, cutting
it into rough chunks. Have ready the boiling water and pour
the teacupful quickly over the butter and lard. Stir with a
knife till the fat has dissolved, and then stir in the flour till
the whole is a not-too-stiff paste. Flour the pastry-board, and
take out two pieces for each tart, a larger and a smaller. Roll
out the larger piece to about the size of a saucer, turn up the
edges all round, about 1 in. high, cover the bottom with
gooseberries, and over this put 1 large dessertspoonful of
Demerara sugar. Take a smaller bit of paste, and roll out
to about the size of a tea-cup, and put over the sugar, pressing
the edges of the pastry well together to prevent the syrup
escaping when cooking. Pinch the edges all round to form
a fluted edge. Cook in a quick oven.

Many people think the edges stand up more perfectly when
cooked, if the tarts are made a day before cooking.

From Mrs. T. Gazard, Gloucestershire.

THREE-DECKER RHUBARB TART

LINE a pie-dish with short pastry, made from ½ lb. flour,
¼ lb. lard and 2 ozs. of butter, salted to taste and mixed
with water. Put in layer of sliced young rhubarb, sprinkle
liberally with sugar and cover with a piece of pastry. Repeat
this until there are three layers of rhubarb. Covering the top
with pastry, cut 3 slits in the centre. Bake in a moderate oven
for 1 hour. The secret in making this tart lies in using plenty

of sugar, so that there is an abundance of sweet syrup when the pie is opened. No water must be added.

Any fruit can be used.

From Mrs. Vincent, Mount Pleasant, Upottery, Devon.

BLACKBERRY COBBLER

1 quart blackberries.	1½ tablespoonfuls castor sugar.
2½ tablespoonfuls milk.	1 tablespoonful lemon juice.
2 cups flour.	1 teaspoonful salt.
5 tablespoonfuls lard.	2 tablespoonfuls butter.
4 teaspoonfuls baking powder (or self-raising flour).	½ cup water.

PLACE the berries, sweetened to taste, in a buttered pie-dish and sprinkle with the lemon juice, and dab with pieces of butter. Rub the lard lightly into the flour, sifted with the baking powder and salt. Stir in the sugar and milk and roll out the paste to the size of the pie-dish. Place on top of the fruit, neatening the edges, which must not come over the brim, and prick with a fork. Bake in a hot oven for ½ hour and serve with custard sauce or cream. This is enough for 6 people, and is delicious.

From Mrs. Godfrey, North Wootton, Shepton Mallet, Somerset.

WINTER TARTS

LINE some tartlet-tins with good short crust; place a little mincemeat in each, then cover with a mixture made by beating together 2 ozs. each butter and sugar, 1 egg, 1 table-spoonful of cake crumbs (rice or Madeira), and a little baking powder; or crumbs of fruit cake may be used and mincemeat left out.

From Mrs. S. E. Hodgson, East Witton, Middleham, Yorkshire.

MIXED FRUIT PIE

WHILE fresh fruit is scarce, the following mixture will be found most economical, and very suitable for pies, or with custard, blancmange, etc.

Take ½ lb. dried apple rings, ¼ lb. dried apricots, cover with water and leave overnight. Next day add about ½ lb. rhubarb, cut fine, and ¼ lb. brown sugar. Cook gently, adding more water if fruit gets too thick, until the apple rings and apricots look clear. Leave to get cold before covering with pie-crust.

From Mrs. F. E. Crisp, Worthwold, Thetford, Norfolk.

TARTS SIONED
(*Welsh Cheesecakes*)

Raspberry jam.

Pastry:

6 ozs. flour.   Salt.
3 ozs. lard.   Cold water.

LINE patty-tins with short crust made with above ingredients.
Put into each a small quantity of raspberry jam, and on the
top of the jam a teaspoonful of the mixture (see below). Bake
immediately in a fairly quick oven till nicely browned. Cool on a
sieve. Before serving sift over with castor sugar.

Mixture:

1 egg and its weight in butter,   A pinch of baking powder.
    sugar and flour.   The grated rind of ½ a lemon.

Beat the butter and sugar to a cream, add flour and egg
alternately (beating well between each addition), then the lemon
rind and, lastly, the baking powder.

From Mary Stokes, Caernarvonshire.

SPICED APPLE CAKE

1 lb. apples.   A little water.
3 ozs. sugar.   Teacupful of cake or biscuit
Rind of ½ lemon.   crumbs.

For the pastry:

3 ozs. flour.   ½ teaspoonful spice.
3 ozs. cornflour.   Yolk of an egg.
2 ozs. butter.   A pinch of salt.
2 ozs. castor sugar.

PUT the apples in a saucepan with sugar, lemon and a little
water. Stew until the apples are reduced to a pulp. Turn
out to cool. To make the pastry: sieve all the dry ingredients
and rub in the butter until fine as breadcrumbs. Bind together
with the egg yolk beaten with a little water. Do not make the
pastry too soft. Knead this until free from cracks, and roll out
thinly.

Grease a tart ring, line it with pastry, sprinkle half the crumbs
at the bottom, fill up with the apple mixture, and cover with the
rest of the crumbs. Roll out the remainder of the pastry and
cover, wetting the edges in the usual way. Bake in a moderate
oven for about 1 hour. Sprinkle with sugar. It is delicious
with custard, cold.

From Mrs. R. Noble, Sewards Farm, Chatteris, Cambs.

Farmhouse Fare

MINCEMEAT AND ALMOND DELIGHT

5 ozs. self-raising flour.
2 ozs. butter.
1 oz. lard.

½ teaspoonful lemon juice.
The yolk of 1 egg.

For the Filling:

4 tablespoonfuls mincemeat.
2 bananas.
2 eggs.
2 ozs. castor sugar.

2 ozs. butter.
2 ozs. ground almonds.
Almonds for decoration.
Almond essence.

SIEVE the flour into a basin, add a pinch of salt, then lightly rub in the lard and butter. Beat the egg yolk, add the lemon juice and 1 tablespoonful of cold water: add gradually to the flour. Mix to a stiff paste, adding more water if required.

For the filling: Cream the butter and sugar together, stir in the beaten eggs, ground almonds, almond essence: mix well.

Line a pie-dish with the pastry; almost fill it with alternate layers of mincemeat and the sliced bananas, then spread the almond mixture on the top. Decorate with the almonds (blanched and halved), bake in a quick oven for ½ hour.

From Mrs. Vincent, Shaugh, Luppitt, Honiton, Devon.

GRAPES IN A PIE

Pastry:

2 cupfuls flour.
1 teaspoonful cream of tartar.
½ teaspoonful bi-carbonate of soda.

½ teaspoonful salt.
4 tablespoonfuls butter.
Milk or water to mix.

Filling:

1 lb. grapes.
½ cupful sugar.
1 tablespoonful lemon juice.

2 tablespoonfuls flour.
1 tablespoonful butter.

MAKE the pastry, using half to line an 8-in. pie-plate. Wash the grapes, and then, using a sharp knife, cut them in half, when the seeds are easily removed. Leave the skins on. Mix the flour and sugar together and sprinkle about half of it over the grapes. Pour over the lemon juice and mix well. Sprinkle the remaining flour and sugar over the bottom of the pastry case (to prevent sogginess). Place the grapes in the case, put dabs of butter here and there on the top and cover with more pastry. Bake for ½ hour to 40 minutes in a moderate oven. Serve hot or cold with fairly thin custard. This makes a delicious sweet.

From Mrs. M. Moulam, Derby.

BREAD, CAKES, BUNS AND BISCUITS

WHITE BREAD

2 lbs. flour.
1 oz. yeast.
1 pint warm milk.

1 oz. sugar.
1 oz. butter or lard.
1 dessertspoonful salt.

CREAM the yeast with a little of the sugar, and add the pint of milk. Mix all dry ingredients. Make a well in the centre, and add half of the fluid. Mix well. Stand in a warm place for ¼ of an hour. When risen add the remainder of the liquid. Knead well. Divide into 2 baking tins. Set aside to rise in a warm atmosphere. Bake for 1 hour.

WHOLEMEAL BREAD

3 lbs. wholemeal flour.
2 lbs. white flour.
Pinch of salt.
2½ pints tepid milk.

2 ozs. lard.
1½ ozs. yeast.
2 mashed potatoes.

RUB the lard into the flour, add the potatoes and salt; mix together; make a well in the flour. Cream the yeast and the sugar and the warm milk, pour into the well, cover with flour, set to rise. Then mix into a dough. Put in tins, keep in a warm place to rise, and bake in a good oven.

Both these recipes from Mrs. K. W. Mollard, Cornwall.

PLANK BREAD

2 lbs. flour.
1 oz. yeast.
1 oz. lard.

1 teaspoonful salt.
1 teaspoonful sugar.
1 breakfastcupful milk and water.

WARM the flour and put into a large bowl, which should have been warmed. Rub the lard into the flour. Put the yeast into a jug with the sugar, and mix with the milk and water, which must be just tepid. Make a well in the centre of the flour and pour in the liquid. Make into a soft dough, cover with a warm cloth and leave it to rise for 1 hour in a warm place, out of the draught. Mould into a large flat cake, kneading and pressing with the hands towards the sides. When shaped it should not be more than 1 in. or 1¼ ins. thick. Leave to rise for 15 minutes. Place carefully on the plank, which should not be too hot. Bake for 20 minutes on one side, then turn and bake for another 20 minutes on the other side.

The plank, or baking-iron of Wales, is placed over the top of a clear fire, and it is important that it should never be made too hot, otherwise the dough will scorch instead of baking slowly and thoroughly.

From Mrs. Owens, Anglesey.

MALT LOAF

½ lb. flour.
¼ lb. sugar.
3 ozs. lard.
2 ozs. sultanas.
1 teaspoonful baking powder.

¼ teaspoonful bi-carbonate of soda.
1 dessertspoonful treacle.
1 egg.
Milk to mix.

MIX all the dry ingredients, rub in the lard, then add the treacle, milk and egg, well beaten. Make a fairly stiff mixture. Bake for about 1 hour in a slow oven.

From Mrs. E. Donaldson, Lancashire.

HEALTH BREAD

1½ lbs. self-raising flour.
1 teacupful granulated sugar.
1 breakfastcupful syrup.
1 egg.

1 breakfastcupful large raisins, stoned.
1 breakfastcupful milk.
A pinch of salt.

MIX flour, sugar and a pinch of salt together and add raisins. Well beat egg and add together with milk. Thoroughly mix all ingredients (sufficient for 2 loaves) and bake in well-greased bread tins in a moderate oven for 1½ hours. After a couple of days the loaf can be buttered and cut into slices, wafer thin, or as required for the menfolk. If kept in a tin cake-bin, these loaves will retain their flavour and moisture for at least a month.

I have made them myself for home use regularly for over 20 years, and they have always been thoroughly enjoyed.

From Mr. John E. Lines, Middlesex.

QUICK MILK ROLLS

½ lb. flour.   ¼ pint milk (sour will do).
2 teaspoonfuls baking powder.   A pinch of salt.

PUT flour, baking powder and salt in basin, pour in milk gradually, and mix into firm dough. Divide into small-sized rolls and brush over the tops with milk. Prick rolls with a fork and place them on greased baking-tin. Bake 10 minutes in a good oven.

From Mrs. J. A. Kimble, Bedfordshire.

APPLE BREAD

A VERY light pleasant bread is made by a mixture of apples and flour in proportion of 1 lb. of apples to 2 lbs. of flour. The usual quantity of yeast is required as in making ordinary bread, and is mixed with flour and warm pulp of apples—after they have been cooked. The dough is allowed to rise for 3 to 4 hours. Then put into long tins, and bake in a moderate oven for about 1 hour to 1¼ hours. Very little water is needed, none generally, if the apples are very fresh.

From Mrs. H. Shirt, Derbyshire.

DATE BREAD

1 lb. dates.   1 lb. flour.
1½ cupfuls boiling water.   ½ lb. sugar.
1½ teaspoonfuls bi-carbonate soda.   2 eggs.
2 ozs. butter.

STONE and cut up the dates, pour over them the boiling water with the bi-carbonate of soda dissolved in it. Leave till cold. Rub the butter into the flour, add the sugar. Beat up the eggs and add to flour with the dates and water. Knead into two loaves and place in well-greased tins. Bake in a moderate oven for 1½ hours.

From Mrs. Livingston, Warwickshire.

" MIXED BREAD "

About 2 lbs. flour   1 teaspoonful cream of tartar.
About ¼ lb. (1 breakfastcup) best   A pinch of salt.
    Indian meal.   Buttermilk.
1 teaspoonful baking soda.

MIX all dry ingredients together, and sift through the fingers to make the dough light. Make into a firm dough with buttermilk (preferably a few days old). Turn on to a floured board, knead and roll out. Cut into farls, and bake on a moderately hot griddle, turning the farls when done on one side and finishing on the other.

This makes a pleasant variety from all-flour and wheaten bread, and is often regarded as quite a novelty. We call it " mixed bread."

Farls are usually about ½ in. thick, and this amount of flour and meal would make 5 or 6 farls, taking about 17 minutes to cook—10 minutes on the first side and 7 minutes after being turned.

From Miss M. Stevenson, Bellevue, Aughnahoory, Kilkeel, Co. Down, N.I.

TREACLE BREAD

2 breakfastcupfuls brown flour.
2 breakfastcupfuls white flour.
½ breakfastcupful sugar.
1 breakfastcupful treacle.
1 breakfastcupful raisins.

Few chopped nuts.
1 egg.
½ pint warm milk.
½ teaspoonful bi-carbonate of soda.

MIX together the flour, sugar, raisins and chopped nuts, then pour the treacle in and mix together well. Add the egg well beaten, then work the warm milk in gradually, leaving a drop to dissolve the bi-carbonate of soda. Stir well and put into greased tins. Bake in a moderate oven for 1½ hours. This amount makes 2 nice-sized loaves and is spread with butter to serve.

From Mrs. Bosworth, The Bridge, Morley, near Derby.

BROWN BREAD (STEAMED)

1 large cup bran.
1 cupful whole meal flour.
2 cupfuls plain flour.
1½ cupfuls thick sour milk.
1 tablespoonful black treacle.

1 tablespoonful sugar.
½ teaspoonful salt.
1 teaspoonful bi-carbonate of soda.
½ cupful sultanas or raisins.

MIX the dry ingredients ; heat the sour milk and add the treacle, mixing well. Stir in the dry ingredients, and lastly the sultanas. Pour into greased tins two-thirds full and steam for 3 hours. Straight marmalade jars are excellent for making, as they turn out nicely shaped and can be cut into dainty rounds to be spread with butter for afternoon tea. Rye flour, oatmeal, Indian corn meal, or any coarse flour can be substituted for the bran.

From Mrs. M. Stokes, Pant Gwyn, Nebo, Penygroes, Caernarvon.

AUSTRALIAN BROWNIE LOAF

3 breakfastcupfuls flour.	2 teaspoonfuls cream of tartar.
1 breakfastcupful brown sugar.	1 cup mixed fruit and peel.
1 teaspoonful mixed spice.	Pinch of salt.
1 teaspoonful bi-carbonate of soda.	Cup of milk, or milk and hot water.

MIX all dry ingredients, then add fruit and mix with the milk until the consistency of dough. Bake in a square bread tin, well greased, in a hot oven for about ¾ hour to 1 hour. Cut in thin slices and butter.

From Mrs. R. R. Watson, Exceat Farm, Seaford, Sussex.

WHOLE-MEAL SPLITS

TAKE 2 breakfastcupfuls whole meal and 1 breakfastcupful white flour ; 1 teaspoonful salt ; mix thoroughly in a basin. Make a well in the middle and into this put 1 teaspoonful sugar, and 1 heaped dessertspoonful yeast. Melt a knob of lard the size of a walnut and mix this with 1 breakfastcupful tepid water to which has been added 1 tablespoonful milk, and pour over the yeast.

Allow to stand till the latter rises and bubbles. Do not knead, but mix with a knife only to the consistency of a soft paste, adding more warm water if necessary. Dust over with flour and set in a warm place to rise well. Then turn out on to a well-floured board, and lightly roll out to less than ½ in. in thickness. Place on a warmed greased tin and set to rise once more. Bake in a moderately hot oven. When cold cut into squares, split and butter and spread with chopped walnut and date, or chopped nuts and cream cheese ; or, if preferred, with butter alone. *From Mrs. M. Johnstone, Benwell, Newcastle-on-Tyne.*

SPECIAL FLOUR FOR SCONES, CAKES, ETC.

4 lbs. flour.	1 oz. bi-carbonate of soda.
2 ozs. cream of tartar.	

SIEVE all together : this makes an excellent self-raising flour and is easy to prepare at home.

From Miss Eleanor Atkinson, Yorkshire.

AUSTRALIAN CHEESE SCONES

TAKE 2 cupfuls sifted flour, ½ cupful grated cheese, 2 tea-spoonfuls baking powder, 1 cupful milk (or buttermilk), a pinch of salt. Mix quickly and cut out. Bake in a hot oven. These are very nice and tasty.

From Mrs. F. Stillborn, Merrijig P.O., via Mansfield, Victoria,
Australia.

POTATO SCONES

3 ozs. cooked potatoes.
3 ozs. flour.
A pinch of salt.

2 level teaspoonfuls baking powder.
1 oz. butter.
Milk (if necessary).

COLD cooked potatoes can be used, but better results are obtained if freshly-boiled ones are rubbed through a sieve before mixing the scones. No milk should be used with freshly-boiled potatoes. Sieve the flour, salt and baking powder in a basin. Rub in the butter with tips of the fingers. Add the sieved potatoes and mix to a fairly soft dough, adding a little milk if necessary. Roll out very lightly to about ¾ in. thick; cut into rounds 2 in. in diameter and bake in a moderate oven until golden brown. Serve hot on a napkin.

From Miss L. Newell, Magherasconse, Ballygowan, Belfast.

WHOLEMEAL DATE TEA-SCONES

1 lb. wheaten-meal.
1 level teaspoonful bread-soda.
1 level teaspoonful cream of tartar.
1 level teaspoonful salt.
3 ozs. butter (or margarine).

6 teaspoonfuls fine sugar.
½ lb. dates, stoned and cut into pieces the size of sultanas.
Buttermilk.

MIX well together the wheaten-meal, bread-soda, cream of tartar and salt. Rub in the shortening, mix in the sugar, add dates and mix. Then add sufficient buttermilk to knead to a firm dough (slightly softer than for bread); cut in triangles and bake in a good oven for about 20 minutes. These are delicious hot with butter for tea.

From Miss E. M. Walker, Ballybrennan, Killinick, Co. Wexford,
Ireland.

HOT CROSS BUNS

1 lb. flour.
Pinch of salt.
¾ oz. yeast.
2 tablespoonfuls castor sugar.
1 level teaspoonful powdered cinnamon.

1 level teaspoonful mixed spice.
2 ozs. margarine.
2 ozs. currants.
1 egg.
About ½ pint milk.

SIEVE flour with salt and spices, rub in fat and add prepared currants. Cream the yeast with a little of the sugar, add a little warm milk and pour in centre of flour, sprinkle lightly over with flour and leave for 10 minutes. Mix to a stiff dough with the beaten egg, adding a little milk if required.

Allow to rise until the mixture doubles itself in size. Divide into portions, mould into small buns, mark with cross, and place on a greased and floured tin. Allow to rise until half as large again. Bake in hot oven 5 to 8 minutes. Melt a little sugar in 1 tablespoonful milk and brush over the buns. This is sufficient to make a dozen buns.

From Miss A. M. Foxley, Glazeley Fields Farm, near Longton, Staffs.

WALNUT AND CINNAMON SCONES

1 lb. flour.
2 teaspoonfuls baking powder.
2 ozs. butter.
1 tablespoonful sugar.
2 tablespoonfuls chopped walnuts.

1 egg.
1 teaspoonful ground cinnamon.
Milk to mix.
Pinch of salt.

MAKE a light scone mixture, roll out quickly. Sprinkle the cinnamon, sugar and nuts over it, fold in three; roll lightly to the required thickness. Cut into shapes and bake in a quick oven.

From Miss Agnes S. Robertson, Thorniehall Farm, Coalburn,
Lanarkshire.

CHEESE MUFFINS

1½ cupfuls flour.
½ cupful grated cheese.
¼ teaspoonful salt.

4 teaspoonfuls baking powder.
1 egg.
¾ cupful milk.

BEAT the egg lightly, add the salt and milk. Sift the flour and baking powder together, and then put in the grated cheese. Make into a dough with the liquid, beat well and roll out. Cut into rounds, brush with beaten egg, and bake for 10 minutes in a sharp oven. These are delicious split, spread with butter and eaten hot.

From Mrs. G. Towler, Yorkshire.

BREAKFAST CHEESE ROLLS

4 teacupfuls sieved flour.
2 tablespoonfuls wheatmeal.
2 teaspoonfuls cream of tartar.
1 teaspoonful baking soda.
1 teaspoonful salt.

4 ozs. castor sugar.
3 ozs. butter.
2 eggs.
Milk.
Some finely-grated cheese.

MIX flour, wheatmeal, salt, cream of tartar, baking soda and sugar together. Lightly rub in the butter. Beat up 2 eggs: reserve some of the beaten egg and milk to brush the rolls. Roll out dough lightly on a floured board to ¼ in. thickness, cut into rounds and brush the edges with milk. Sprinkle on the finely-grated cheese, fold over double, brush with egg and milk. Bake on a buttered baking-sheet in a hot oven for 15 minutes.

From Miss Mary MacDonald, Brackley, Gollanfield, Inverness-shire.

PIKELETS

1 lb. flour.	Pinch of salt.
1 oz. yeast.	2 eggs.
1 teaspoonful castor sugar.	Rather more than 1 pint of milk.

MIX the sugar and yeast together until liquid; next add the warmed milk. Make a hole in the flour, add the salt, pour in the liquid and mix well; then add the beaten eggs and beat the batter well for 10 minutes. Put in a warm place to rise, which will take about 1 hour, then cook the pikelets either in the oven or over the fire. If in the oven, heat the baking-tin and brush it over with melted dripping. Put 1 large tablespoonful of the mixture at equal distances on the greased tin, turn them once when holes have formed on the surface, butter them and serve hot.

To cook over the fire, melt some fat in the pan, then drop the mixture in tablespoonfuls at equal distances in the hot fat. Five or 6 pikelets can be cooked at once in this way. Turn over once and brown the other side. These are delicious for tea, but any left over may be toasted and buttered the next day.

From Mrs. M. Lingard, The Mill House, North Kelsey, Lincoln.

WELSH CAKES

| 1 lb. self-raising flour. | ½ lb. currants. |
| ½ lb. butter or lard. | ½ teaspoonful salt. |

MIX the butter, or lard, and the flour well together with the hands, then add the sugar and currants. Take 1 egg and beat it in a basin, then put in the salt and a cup of milk. Mix into the dry ingredients (using a fork) until it is just stiff. Finish with the hands.

Then put your iron pan over the fire to get warm and rub it over with lard. While the iron is warming roll out your cakes and cut with a cup. Put them on the pan and leave until brown one side, then turn and leave them for 5 minutes and they will be done. The fire should not be too sharp.

From Mrs. L. K. Davies, Montgomeryshire.

BANBURY CAKES

Flaky pastry.

¼ lb. butter.	¼ oz. ground cinnamon.
½ lb. finely-cut mixed candied peel.	¼ oz. mixed spice.
1 lb. currants.	A little lemon juice.

MAKE the pastry and allow to stand for 1 hour. Beat the butter to a cream, mix in the candied peel, currants, cinnamon, mixed spice and lemon juice. Mix all well together. Roll out the pastry about ½ in. thick and cut into pieces, then roll out again until each piece becomes twice the size, put some filling in the middle of one side, fold the other over it, and pinch it up into a somewhat oval shape. Flatten at the top, letting the seam be at the bottom. Brush the tops over with white of egg and sprinkle on granulated sugar.

From Mrs. B. Manley, Oxfordshire.

YORKSHIRE PARKIN

1½ lbs. medium oatmeal.
¾ lb. flour.
1 tablespoonful sugar.
1 teaspoonful ground ginger.
2 lbs. treacle.

¼ lb. butter and dripping.
1 small teaspoonful salt.
1 teaspoonful bi-carbonate of soda.
¼ pint milk.

MIX all the dry ingredients together. Warm the treacle and dripping together and dissolve the bi-carbonate of soda in the slightly warm milk and mix all well together. Grease a large pudding-tin or 2 smaller ones and bake in a moderate oven for about ¾ hour, or until it is just firm to the touch.

Mrs. A. Cooper, Home Farm, Follifoot, Harrogate, Yorkshire.

HOT APPLE MUFFINS

3 large cooking apples.
8 ozs. flour.
3 ozs. lard.
1 teaspoonful baking powder.

1 egg.
2 ozs. moist sugar.
A little castor sugar.
A little butter.

MIX baking powder and flour together, rub in the lard and add the moist sugar. Peel, core and mince the apples. Beat the egg well and, with the minced apples, add to the flour, etc. Work all well together and add a little milk if too dry, but on no account should it be too wet, as apples moisten it in baking. Put into a greased flat tin and bake in a moderate oven. When done, cut in rounds, split open and butter, dusting with castor sugar before serving. Time for cooking: about ½ hour.

From Miss H. Tibbs, Somersetshire.

GREAT GRANNIE'S GINGERBREADS

1 lb. flour.
½ lb. treacle.
½ lb. sugar

½ lb. fresh butter.
½ oz. good ginger.

MIX 24 hours before baking, place a piece of candied peel on each biscuit, and bake in a quick oven. If preferred, add 1 or 2 drops of essence of lemon and a dust of baking powder.

From Miss N. I. Saunders, Suffolk.

APPLE GINGERBREAD WITH CINNAMON ICING

½ lb. cooking apples.
3 ozs. Demerara sugar.
¼ lb. golden syrup.
3 ozs. butter.

6 ozs. self-raising flour.
1 teaspoonful ground ginger.
¼ teaspoonful ground cloves.
1 egg.

PEEL and slice apples, and put in a pan with 1 dessertspoonful sugar, and just sufficient water to keep them from burning. Stew gently until tender. Mash up and leave to get cold. Put the golden syrup in a pan with the butter, and the remainder of the sugar; dissolve slowly then leave to cool.

Sift the flour into a basin with the ground ginger and ground cloves. Whisk up the egg, add the dissolved syrup and fat, etc., and whisk together; then add to the flour. Mix well, stir in the apple pulp and beat all together. Turn into a well-greased oblong tin. Bake in a moderate oven, about ½ hour. When cooked, let stand for a little before turning out of tin. The icing is optional.

CINNAMON ICING

6 ozs. icing sugar.
2 to 3 dessertspoonfuls water.

1 level teaspoonful ground cinnamon.

RUB sugar through a sieve mix with the ground cinnamon. Then stir in sufficient moderately hot water to make a thick coating consistently. Spread on top of gingerbread and leave to set.

From Miss Mary MacDonald, Brackley, Gollanfield, Inverness-shire.

CRYSTALLIZED GINGER CAKE

3 ozs. butter.
3 ozs. castor sugar.
6 ozs. self-raising flour.
1 dessertspoonful golden syrup.

2 ozs. crystallized ginger.
¼ teaspoonful ground ginger.
2 eggs.

BEAT the sugar, butter and golden syrup to a cream. Sift the flour and ground ginger together. Sprinkle a handful of flour over the mixture, add 1 egg and beat all well together. Add more flour and the second egg, and beat well again. If more moisture is needed, use a little milk or hot water: add the remainder of the flour. Finally, add the grated crystallized ginger and beat the mixture well. Put into a well-greased and lined cake-tin. Bake in a moderate oven until golden brown and firm (about 45 to 50 minutes). This is a delicious cake and one which does not go dry. " Cargo " ginger is cheaper than other crystallized ginger.

From Miss L. N. Wood, Manor House, Mollington, near Banbury.

GINGER BREADS

2 lbs. flour.
1 lb. moist sugar.
1 lb. syrup.
1½ ozs. ground ginger.
1 oz. cassia.

1 teaspoonful mace.
A little orange peel.
2 tablespoonfuls bi-carbonate of soda.
1 lb butter.

MIX flour, sugar and spices all together. Rub butter in and mix with the syrup into a firm ball. Pinch off pieces the size of a walnut, and put on a sheet, about 12 at a time, and bake in a moderate oven. This amount will make about 7 or 8 dozen ginger breads which are very tasty.

From Mrs. K. E. Mollard, Rose Down Farm, Camborne, Cornwall.

GINGER SHORTBREAD

2 breakfastcupfuls of flour.
1 breakfastcupful of *moist brown* sugar (this is important as white sugar won't make it).
½ lb. butter.

2 teaspoonfuls ground ginger.
1 small teaspoonful bi-carbonate of soda.
Pinch of salt.

MIX all dry ingredients together, work in the butter until the whole becomes crumbly. Spread evenly in a well-greased dripping-tin and bake in a moderate oven for ¾ hour. Cut into fingers while warm and lift gently from tin with knife-blade.

This is an economical shortbread which is quickly made, and is a good stand-by as it keeps well in tins.

From Mrs. M. E. Glover, Lane Head Farm, Brough, Westmorland.

LEMON DIGESTIVE CAKE

12 ozs. any good cake flour.
1 lemon.
2 ozs. each lard and butter.

2 eggs.
½ teaspoonful ground ginger
½ gill milk.

SIFT flour and ginger, rub in fats, beat the yolks and 1 white of the eggs and stir into the flour with the milk. Then stir in the second egg white, beaten stiffly. Do not beat the mixture. Half fill a shallow tin, greased and lined with paper, and bake in a very moderate oven for about 1 hour. Cool on a sieve. This makes a very light cake.

From Mrs. Rogers, Acton Park, Wrexham.

BANANA FINGERS

MIX together ½ lb. rolled oats, ½ lb. sugar, ½ lb. wholemeal flour, ½ lb. butter and ½ teaspoonful bi-carbonate of soda or 1 teaspoonful baking powder. Mix to a stiff dough with 2 eggs. Divide in two portions, putting one in the bottom of a greased shallow tin, about 9 in. square. Slice 4 bananas on to this, then put the other half of the mixture on top. Bake a golden brown and cut into fingers. Walnuts or chopped almonds can be used instead of bananas. Excellent for school lunches or picnics.

From Miss H. Rowlinson, East Feldy, Aston-by-Budworth,
near Northwich, Cheshire.

BARA BRITH

1 lb. self-raising flour.
½ lb. brown sugar.
¼ lb. lard or butter.
½ lb. currants or sultanas.
1 teaspoonful egg powder.
1 lemon.

1 teaspoonful carraway seeds, if liked.
Salt and spice to taste.
1 teaspoonful bi-carbonate of soda.
1 large tablespoonful of treacle.
½ pint buttermilk.

MIX fat well into flour, add sugar, egg powder, grated rind of lemon, fruit, salt, spice and (last of all) juice of lemon and treacle. Mix all well together with the bi-carbonate of soda in the buttermilk. Put into a bread-tin and bake 1¾ to 2 hours.

From Miss A. M. Davies, Montgomeryshire.

STEAMED CHOCOLATE CAKE
(*Without Eggs*)

WELL mix 2 cupfuls plain flour, ½ teaspoonful bi-carbonate of soda, 1 tablespoonful sugar, 1½ tablespoonfuls cocoa or chocolate powder; rub in 2 ozs. fat, 2 tablespoonfuls golden syrup, milk (sweet or sour) to make into a stiff batter. Have ready a well-greased cake-tin, put in mixture, cover top with greased paper, place in steamer, cook 1¼ hours; then place in warm oven for 10 minutes to dry off the top. Not to be cut until next day.

From Miss J. Hocking, White House Farm, Alton, Hants.

AN ECONOMICAL FARMHOUSE CURRANT CAKE

2 lbs. self-raising flour.
¾ lb. sugar.
½ lb. lard and butter mixed.
¼ lb. currants.

¼ lb. sultanas.
¼ lb. peel.
1 beaten egg with milk enough to make the mixture stiff.

RUB the lard and butter into the flour, add the sugar and fruit, and mix with the beaten egg and milk into a stiff mixture. Put into 3 loaf tins and bake in a moderate oven for ¾ hour. Sufficient to make 3 cakes.

From Mrs. Joyce Noden, Walnut Tree Farm, Alvanley, Helsby,
near Warrington.

GRASMERE SHORTCAKE

½ lb. flour.
¼ lb. moist brown sugar.
¼ teaspoonful baking soda.

¼ lb. butter.
½ teaspoonful ground ginger.

Filling:

¼ lb. icing sugar.
2 ozs. butter.
½ teaspoonful ground ginger.

A small quantity of chopped preserved bottle ginger.
1 teaspoonful of the syrup.

PLACE the dry ingredients in a bowl and rub in the butter until it has the consistency of breadcrumbs. Have ready a shallow baking-tin lined with greased paper and empty the mixture into it. Spread evenly with the hand and press very lightly together. Bake in a very moderate oven until nicely browned. Turn out and trim the edges. Cut in two while still hot.

This can be kept in an airtight tin till required, when it makes a delicious and unusual cake with the filling.

To make the filling, beat the butter and sugar to a cream, and add the chopped ginger and syrup. Spread evenly on one of the pieces of cake and press the other into position on top.

From Mrs. J. Little, Cumberland.

SCRUGGIN CAKE

1 lb. self-raising flour.
¾ lb. chopped scruggins.

½ lb. granulated sugar.
Milk and water for mixing.

CHOP the scruggins into small pieces, then put in a basin the flour, chopped scruggins and sugar; mix all the dry ingredients together, then make into a soft dough with the milk and water. Roll out the dough about 1 in. thick and press into a square tin, well greased with lard. Cut the top of the cake into squares, and sprinkle with a little castor sugar, bake in a moderate oven for about ½ hour.

Mrs. W. Sadler, Meend Farm, Penalt, Lydart, near Monmouth.

BUTTERMILK CAKE

1 lb. flour.
½ lb. brown sugar.
1 lb. mixed fruit.
½ lb. butter.
1 teaspoonful bi-carbonate of soda.

A little cinnamon.
Mixed spice and ground ginger.
1 tablespoonful black treacle.
Nearly ½ pint buttermilk or sour milk.

RUB butter into flour until dry and crumbly. Add sugar, fruit and flavouring; warm the buttermilk and to it add the treacle and soda. Mix this till it froths. Stir and bake in a brisk oven.

From Miss K. Hall, Moyrusk, Moira, Co. Down.

DATE AND WALNUT CAKE

12 ozs. flour.
½ oz. sugar.
1 teaspoonful baking powder.
½ oz. butter.
4 ozs. walnuts.

1 lb. dates, cut small.
1 teaspoonful bi-carbonate of soda
    in a teacupful of cold milk.
1 egg.

CREAM the butter and sugar, add the egg, then the flour, dates, walnuts. Mix with the milk and bi-carbonate of soda, beat well, then mix in baking powder. Bake in a flat, well-greased tin for 1½ hours.

From Mrs. Bell, Meadow House, Mains, Nutton, Berwick-on-Tweed.

FIG SLY CAKES

6 ozs. cooking figs.
3 ozs. chopped walnuts.
1½ ozs. currants.

1½ ozs. raisins.
2 ozs. sugar.
Water.

Pastry :

8 ozs. flour.
3 ozs. lard.
3 ozs. butter.

2 ozs. castor sugar.
Pinch of salt.

MAKE filling by chopping figs and walnuts with currants and raisins. Add sugar and simmer, in sufficient water to cover, until tender and pulpy. Allow to cool. For the pastry, mix flour, sugar and salt, and light rub in the shortening. Mix to a paste with cold water. Put in a cool place for about 1 hour. Roll out pastry and line tin—a toffee-tray size is suitable. Spread in filling and cover with pastry. Seal edges and mark with back of knife, then brush with egg yolk and milk. Bake in a fairly hot oven for 20 to 30 minutes. When cool cut into squares.

From Mrs. E. Rutherford, Tweedmouth.

WIMBLEDON CAKE

1 lb. flour.
½ lb. butter.
½ lb. sugar.
½ lb. currants.
2 ozs. chopped candied peel.

1 teaspoonful mixed spice.
½ pint sour milk.
1 teaspoonful bi-carbonate of soda.
1 tablespoonful syrup.

RUB the butter into the flour; add the sugar, currants, peel and spice. Warm the syrup and stir it into the milk, add the soda and mix all together. Bake in a greased dripping-tin in a moderate oven for 1½ hours.

From Miss M. C. Utley, Watchet, Somerset.

COVENTRY GODCAKES

12 ozs. plain flour.
12 ozs. margarine.
Pinch of salt.
Water to mix.

Mincemeat.
1 white of egg.
Castor sugar.

ADD a pinch of salt to the flour and sieve into basin, pour in cold water gradually and mix it to a stiff paste. It should be neither sticky nor dry, just pliable. Turn on to a floured board and knead lightly until smooth. Roll out to an oblong shape. Press out the margarine until not quite half the size of the pastry, put on the one half and fold over the other.

Press edges well together, roll out to same thickness as before, fold into three; do this twice more, but the last time roll out to about $\frac{1}{8}$ in. thick. Cut out three-cornered pieces of pastry and place mincemeat in centre, place another piece of pastry on top, press well together, and make one or two cuts on top and bake in a very hot oven for about 15 minutes.

When cooked, glaze the tops with the white of egg beaten to a froth and dust castor sugar over. Return to oven for 3 minutes. Place on a sieve until cold.

These cakes are sold round here for New Year's Day in most confectioners' shops, and they are also made at the old-fashioned farmhouses. They vary in size up to 18 in. per side. Jolly good they are. God-parents usually present one to their god-children for good luck. *From Miss N. Fennell, Warwickshire.*

FRUIT CAKES

Filling:

$\frac{1}{2}$ lb. currants or seedless raisins.
$\frac{1}{2}$ lb. rhubarb.

1 cupful sugar.
Piece of butter the size of a walnut.

Put above mixture into a small pan and stew gently till soft. Allow to cool.

Paste:

$\frac{1}{2}$ lb. self-raising flour.
1 teaspoonful sugar.

$\frac{1}{4}$ lb. butter or lard.

RUB the butter into the flour and sugar and make into a stiff paste with a little water. Roll out, divide in two and place one half on a shallow baking-tin (a roast-tin does quite well). Spread on the mixture and place other half on top. Brush with white of egg (or milk with sugar dissolved in it). Bake for $\frac{1}{2}$ an hour in a brisk oven. When cool sprinkle with sugar and cut into 16 pieces. *From Mrs. R. Weir, Berwickshire.*

CARAWAY ANGEL CAKE

5 ozs. flour.
4 ozs. castor sugar.
2 ozs. butter.
1 gill milk.

The whites of 2 eggs.
1 teaspoonful baking powder.
2 ozs. candied peel.
1 large teaspoonful caraway seeds.

BEAT the butter and sugar to a soft cream, stir in the milk gradually, and when it is quite smooth add the stiffly-whipped whites of eggs. Mix the baking powder and a pinch of salt with the flour, and stir it in lightly, then the candied peel thinly sliced and the caraway seeds. Pour into a well-greased tin and bake 1¼ hours in a moderate oven.

This is a useful recipe when egg yolks are used to make a custard. *From Miss J. Haile, Hetton-le-Hole, Durham.*

GINGER CAKE

1 lb. flour.
6 ozs. lard.
1 cupful sour milk.
½ lb. granulated sugar.
2 teaspoonfuls ground ginger.

Pinch of salt.
1 teaspoonful bi-carbonate of soda.
1 tablespoonful boiling water.
1 cupful black treacle.

CREAM the lard and sugar together, add the treacle and sour milk, then the bi-carbonate of soda dissolved in boiling water. Sift together the ginger, salt and flour; beat them into the mixture. Line a flat oblong tin with well-greased grease-proof paper, and bake in a moderate oven for 40 minutes.
From Mrs. Violet Cooper, Dennis Farm, St. Columb, Cornwall.

CHOCOLATE TARGETS

3 ozs. castor sugar.
1 oz. cocoa.

2 ozs. butter.

CREAM these together, warming the basin if too stiff to spread. Roll out about ¾ lb. of rather firm short pastry into a strip 12 in. by 9 in., spread on the above mixture. Roll up as for a jam roll, wetting the last edge to hold it in place. Cut into 12 slices and lay flat on a baking-tin. Bake for about 20 minutes in a moderate oven.
From Mrs. W. Proctor, The Church Farm, Lessingham, Norwich, Norfolk.

JAM CAKE

8 ozs. flour.
2 ozs. sugar.
2 ozs. lard.

2 ozs. butter.
½ teaspoonful salt.
1 egg.

MIX the dry ingredients, rub in the lard and butter lightly and mix into a stiff paste with the beaten egg and a little milk if necessary. Divide into two parts and roll out thinly (both the same size). Cover one with raspberry jam. Place the other on top and nip together. Place on a greased baking-sheet and bake in a moderate oven for 15 to 20 minutes. When cool, cut into dainty shapes.

From Mrs. M. Stokes, Pant Gwyn Nebo, Penygroes, Caernarvon.

OLD ENGLISH CIDER CAKE

¼ lb. butter.	1 teaspoonful bi-carbonate of soda.
4 ozs. sugar.	½ a nutmeg, well grated.
2 eggs.	1 teacupful cider.
8 ozs. flour.	

BEAT the butter and sugar to a cream. Add the eggs, well beaten, then 4 ozs. flour sifted with the bi-carbonate of soda, and the nutmeg. Pour over all the cider beaten to a froth, and mix thoroughly. Stir in the other 4 ozs. flour and mix well together. Bake in a shallow well-greased tin in a moderate oven for 45 minutes. This cake when properly made is delicious, with a distinctive flavour.

From Mrs. J. Preston, Oxfordshire.

VINEGAR CAKE

1 lb. flour.	¼ lb. stoned raisins.
½ lb. sugar.	3 tablespoonfuls vinegar.
½ lb. butter and dripping.	1 teaspoonful bi-carbonate of soda
½ lb. currants.	Just over ¼ pint of milk.

RUB fat well into the flour, add fruit and sugar. Put the milk into a large jug, and add the vinegar. Mix the bi-carbonate of soda with a little milk and pour it into the milk and vinegar quickly, taking care to hold the jug over the cake mixture, as it will froth up. Stir into the flour, fruit, etc., put into a well-greased tin and bake in a hot oven for the first ½ hour, then a cooler one.

From Mrs. H. Huggins, Norfolk.

GOLDEN BETTYS

3 ozs. sugar.	¼ teaspoonful bi-carbonate of soda.
2 ozs. butter.	¼ teaspoonful cream of tartar.
4 ozs. flour.	2 tablespoonfuls milk.
2 teaspoonfuls melted syrup.	1 egg.
1 teaspoonful ground ginger.	

BEAT the butter and sugar to a cream, and add melted syrup, then the beaten egg ; and beat well. Add the rest of the ingredients gradually. Half fill well-greased patty-tins, and bake in a moderate oven 15 to 20 minutes.

From Mrs. G. Thom, Tombreck, Glenbuchat, by Alford, Aberdeenshire.

D

WHEATEN FRUIT CAKES

Wheaten Pastry:

½ lb. wheaten meal (finely ground).
Pinch of salt.
½ teaspoonful baking soda.
1 teaspoonful cream of tartar.

¼ lb. butter.
Teaspoonful sugar.
Water to mix.

Filling:

½ lb. seedless raisins.
2 apples (about ½ lb.).
Piece of butter the size of a walnut.

2 tablespoonfuls brown sugar.
1 teaspoonful ground cinnamon.
2 tablespoonfuls water.

MIX dry ingredients in a bowl; rub in butter and mix with a little water into short crust pastry. Divide in two portions, and roll out each to form 9-in. square. Prepare the filling the previous day if possible so as to have it cold. Grate the apples or put them through a mincer, add other ingredients and simmer slowly till liquid is absorbed. Spread filling on one square of pastry and place other on top. Bake in moderate oven for ½ hour after brushing top with milk in which a little sugar is dissolved. When cool, sprinkle sugar on top and cut into 16 small squares.

From Mrs. R. Weir, Ladyflat, Duns, Berwickshire.

OAT CAKE

½ lb. bread dough.
¼ lb. fine oatmeal.

2 ozs. good bacon dripping or lard.

MIX all together into a smooth paste. Roll out very thin on to baking-tins. Mark into squares and prick well with a fork. Bake in a moderate oven until nice and crisp. This is delicious spread with fresh butter.

From Mrs. E. Moore, Sandford Drigg, Holmrook, Cumberland.

OATMEAL COOKIES

2 cupfuls flour.
2 cupfuls oatmeal.
2 tablespoonfuls lard or margarine.
1 cupful brown sugar.

1 teaspoonful soda.
1 teaspoonful salt.
¼ teaspoonful cinnamon and nutmeg.

RUB the lard or margarine into the flour and oatmeal. Mix all with a little water, not too soft, then roll out thin and cut into cake size. These cookies are good with a date filling.

For date filling, boil dates for 10 minutes in a little water and then put between layers of paste and bake quickly until browned. About ½ lb. of dates is sufficient.

From Miss Margaret Ferguson, Ireland.

" SINGIN' HINNY " or
NORTHUMBERLAND FARMHOUSE GIRDLE CAKE

¾ lb. flour.	3 ozs. currants.
2 ozs. ground rice.	1 teaspoonful salt.
2 ozs. sugar.	2 teaspoonfuls baking powder.
1 oz. lard.	1 gill liquid, half cream and half milk.

MIX flour, ground rice, salt, sugar and baking powder. Rub in lard. Mix in currants which have been previously washed and dried. Then add the liquid and mix to a moderately soft dough. Roll this out to a ¼-in. thickness. Prick all over with a fork and bake on a fairly hot girdle until nicely browned on both sides. It can be cut in halves or quarters for convenience in turning. This cake is delicious split and buttered and eaten hot. *From Miss Mary J. Bell, Northumberland.*

WILTSHIRE LARDY CAKE

A half-quartern of dough from the baker.	Granulated sugar.
	Mixed spice if liked.
Lard.	

ROLL the dough on a floured pastry-board. On it put dabs of lard about the size of a walnut and about 1½ ins. apart. Sprinkle with granulated sugar. Fold into three from the ends, and then into three from the sides. Turn to the right and roll out again. Repeat this process twice, each time putting on dabs of lard. After three foldings and lardings, roll out to size of baking-tin, score across and across with a knife, and bake in a moderate oven. If liked, mixed spice may be mixed with the sugar, and currants or sultanas may be added as well. This cake is sometimes called " Shaley Cake " by the older people, and is usually served hot for tea on Saturdays or Sundays.

From Miss Doris Hiskins, Wiltshire.

WHEEL CAKES

THESE cakes are delicious for tea and may be served either hot or cold.

Put 1 cupful currants, 1 cupful sultanas, ½ cupful sugar, 1 teaspoonful mixed spice and a little water in a small pan, and simmer slowly for 10 minutes, stirring occasionally. Remove from fire to cool. Mix 2 cupfuls flour, 2 tablespoonfuls sugar, 1 teaspoonful each baking soda and cream of tartar, and rub in 2 ozs. margarine until like fine breadcrumbs. Mix with buttermilk to a soft dough. Roll out into a large piece, spread the mixture over evenly, roll up like a roly-poly, and use a floured knife to cut into slices ½ in. thick. Place on a greased baking-sheet, brush over with milk and bake in a hot oven for 20 minutes.

From Miss Agnes Campbell, Ouley Hill, Ardarragh, Newry, Co. Down.

HONEY BRAN KNOBS

2 cupfuls flour.
⅔ cupful butter.
½ cupful brown sugar.
½ cupful honey.
½ cupful stoned raisins.
Vanilla essence to taste.
2½ cupfuls bran.

⅔ cupful milk.
½ cupful chopped nuts.
2 eggs.
¾ teaspoonful bi-carbonate of soda.
½ teaspoonful salt.
1 teaspoonful baking powder.
1 teaspoonful cinnamon.

SIEVE together the flour, baking powder, cinnamon and salt. Melt the butter, add the sugar, honey and eggs (well beaten), mixing together in a bowl. Dissolve the soda in the milk, then to the mixture in the bowl add the sifted dry ingredients alternately with the milk. Stir in the raisins, nuts, bran and vanilla essence. Mix all well together and drop by teaspoonfuls on to a well-greased baking-sheet. Bake 10 minutes in a fairly hot oven. *From Mrs. V. Cantwell, Hampshire.*

DOUGHNUTS FOR LENT

1 large cupful granulated sugar.
1 large cupful milk.
2 ozs. butter.
2 small eggs.

A good sprinkling of currants.
1½ teaspoonfuls cream of tartar.
¼ teaspoonful bi-carbonate of soda.

MIX all dry ingredients well, then add milk and beaten eggs and enough flour to make a nice soft, workable paste. Roll into small balls (they will double their size) and fry in deep fat till a nice nut-brown. Toss in sugar. This quantity will make a good number.

From Margaret Coleman, Reed End, Therfield, Royston, Herts.

CORN GRIDDLE CAKES

1 cupful flour.
½ cupful wheatmeal.
1¼ cupfuls milk.

3 tablespoonfuls sugar.
1 egg.
¾ cupful drained canned maize.
3 teaspoonfuls baking powder.

SIFT together flour, meal, baking powder, sugar and salt. Beat egg, add to milk and stir in maize. Mix lightly with dry ingredients, then beat well. Bake in large tablespoonfuls on a greased girdle, keeping the batter as round as possible as you drop it. When bubbles show on top and they are lightly brown underneath, turn cakes and cook lightly on the other side. Serve buttered, hot. If preferred, you can omit the sugar, season with pepper and salt, and serve with hot bacon or sausages.

From Mrs. Mary Stokes, Caernarvonshire.

COCO-NUT OAT BISCUITS

¼ lb. flour.
¼ lb. coco-nut.
2 ozs. lard.
¼ lb. sugar.
¼ lb. rolled oats.

2 ozs. margarine.
1 tablespoonful golden syrup.
2 tablespoonfuls water.
1 teaspoonful bi-carbonate of soda.

MIX the dry ingredients together. Rub in the fat and dissolve the bi-carbonate of soda in the water. Mix with the hand. Roll out on a floured board and cut into shapes with cutter. Bake in a cool oven until a nice biscuit colour.

From Martha Annie Bradley, Yorkshire.

DIGESTIVE BISCUITS

4 ozs. medium oatmeal.
1½ ozs. castor sugar.
4 ozs. wholemeal flour.
3 ozs. butter.

A pinch of salt.
A small pinch of bi-carbonate of soda.
½ an egg.

RUB butter into flour and oatmeal, add sugar, salt and soda. Bind with the beaten egg, put the dough on pastry board sprinkled with oatmeal, and roll out. Sprinkle lightly with oatmeal, roll it in, and then cut in oval shapes. Bake in a tin in a fairly hot oven.

From Mrs. M. Ware, Gloucestershire.

BRANDY SNAP

¼ lb. butter.
½ lb. treacle.
¼ lb. sugar.
½ lb. flour.

1 tablespoonful ground ginger.
Rind and juice of 1 lemon.
1 teaspoonful ground cinnamon.

MELT butter in a jar with the treacle and sugar. Mix the flour with ground ginger, the grated rind and the juice of 1 lemon, and the ground cinnamon. Mix with the melted butter and treacle, beat together 5 minutes, bake in a very slow oven until a pale brown, roll quickly on small rolling-pin or handle of wooden spoon.

From Mrs. Edith Laughton, Cherry Willingham, near Lincoln.

ORANGE TEA BISCUITS

2 cupfuls flour.
½ cupful shortening (mixed butter
  and lard is best).

4 teaspoonfuls baking powder.
¾ cupful cold milk or half milk and
  half water.

SIFT together the dry ingredients, rub in the shortening and
mix with the liquid to a soft dough. Toss the dough on
to a floured board and handle as little as possible. Roll or pat
to about ¾ in. thick and cut out with a floured biscuit cutter.
Dip lumps of sugar into orange juice (or lemon juice) and press
a lump into the top of each biscuit before putting them into
a hot oven for 12 to 15 minutes. (Probably half a lump of cane
sugar would be sufficient. Our beet sugar lumps are smaller.
Also I use less baking powder than the recipe calls for, as most
recipes on this continent use more than is necessary.)

The biscuit recipe lends itself to infinite variety. Mix in
grated cheese or diced crisped bacon for savoury biscuits—
currants, raisins, dates, spices, fresh berries, etc., for sweet
ones. A " pie " crust made of tiny round biscuits placed close
together on top of the meat or fowl is dainty and economical.

From Mrs. Alan Cole, Canada.

CHEESE BISCUITS

6 ozs. plain flour.
4 ozs. butter.
2 ozs. grated cheese.

Pepper and salt to taste.
A little milk for mixing.

RUB fat into flour, add cheese, which must be finely grated,
pepper and salt. Mix to a stiff paste with cold milk and
roll to about ⅛ in. thickness. Cut into rounds about the size of
the top of a tumbler, prick with a fork to prevent rising, and
bake in a hot oven 7 to 10 minutes. The biscuits should be a
light golden brown when done.

From Miss J. Griffiths, Golfa, Welshpool.

RICH BUTTER BISCUITS

1 lb. flour.
½ lb. butter.
⅓ lb. sugar.
2 eggs.

A pinch of salt.
½ cup milk.
1 teaspoonful baking powder.
¼ lb. sultanas.

SIFT the flour, salt and baking powder into a bowl. Rub in
the butter. Stir in the sugar and fruit and mix to a smooth
dough with beaten eggs and milk. Roll out and cut with shaped
pastry cutters. Bake in a hot oven. When cool, store in an
airtight tin. *From Miss E. Tudor, Palman, Lower Bebington, Wirral.*

SAUCES, PICKLES, CHUTNEYS

MUSTARD PICKLE

¼ lb. tin mustard.
1 cup fresh butter.
1 cup sugar.
2 ozs. flour.
1 oz. turmeric.
1 quart vinegar.
1 head cauliflower.

1 quart small onions.
1 quart sliced onions.
1 quart green tomatoes.
1 quart kidney beans.
1 quart sliced cucumber.
1 cup nasturtium seeds.
1 teaspoonful celery seed.

PUT all the vegetables into salt water overnight: in the morning strain them and boil in weak salt water until tender (a little underdone rather than overdone). Have the sauce, made with the mustard, butter, sugar, flour, turmeric and vinegar, ready in a double boiler.

Mix the flour, sugar and turmeric with the vinegar, and when the vinegar is very hot add the butter, stirring all the time. Add the mustard last after taking the mixture from the fire. Put the pickles into a large basin and cover with the hot sauce. Mix well and tie down with a cloth. After 3 days make a second lot of sauce, like the first, adding a little more sugar and 1½ ozs. turmeric. Mix thoroughly.

From Mrs. E. Hyatt, Bosworth Cross Roads, Measham, Burton-on-Trent.

PICCALILLI

2 cauliflowers.
2 medium-sized cucumbers.
16 French beans (young).
1 lb. onions.
1 medium-sized marrow.
1 quart vinegar.

1 oz. whole spice.
¼ lb. Demerara sugar.
½ oz. ground ginger.
1 oz. mustard.
½ oz. turmeric.
1 tablespoonful flour.

CUT the vegetables into small pieces, lay on a dish, and sprinkle with salt. Leave for 12 hours. Drain off water, boil nearly all the vinegar with the spice, then strain. Mix the other ingredients, with the remaining cold vinegar, into a smooth paste; then mix with boiled vinegar. Pour into saucepan, add vegetables, and boil for 15 minutes.

From Miss I. Underwood, Hertfordshire.

DATE PICKLE

2 lbs. dates (stoned).   2 ozs. pickling spice.
1¼ pints vinegar.   Pinch of salt.

BOIL the vinegar and spice together and pour over the dates while hot. Place in jars and tie down. This pickle is ready for use in 3 months.

From Mrs. A. Lount, Rutlandshire.

FIG PICKLE

1 lb. dried figs (cooking).

Pickling mixture :

½ pint vinegar.   1 dessertspoonful ground cinna-
1 lb. Demerara sugar.   mon.
1 dessertspoonful ground cloves.   1 teaspoonful ground mace.
                                   1 teaspoonful allspice.

WASH 1 lb. of figs in cold water. Leave them to soak over-night in a basin just covered with cold water. The next day drain them in a colander. For the pickling mixture, boil the sugar and vinegar till it is thick, then add cloves, cinnamon, ground mace and allspice. Simmer for a minute or two, then add the figs and cook very gently for 1 hour. Put into jars and cover. It is delicious with pork, cold meat or cold bacon.

From Mrs. A. Williams, Monmouthshire.

PICKLED EGGS

16 hard-boiled eggs.   ½ oz. allspice.
1 quart vinegar.   ½ oz. ginger (whole).
½ oz. black peppercorns.

REMOVE eggshells and place eggs in wide-necked jars. Boil the peppercorns, spice and ginger in the vinegar for 10 minutes; pour it, while boiling hot, over the eggs. When cold cover closely and store in a cool dry place.

These are ready for use in about a fortnight and are delicious when eaten with cold meat or cheese.

From Mrs. J. C. Beakley, Cambridgeshire.

BLACKBERRY PICKLE

1 quart blackberries.   1½ ozs. allspice.
1 pint white vinegar.   ½ oz. ground ginger.
2 lbs. sugar.

STEEP the blackberries and ginger for 12 hours. Then bring the vinegar to the boil. Add the berries and boil for ½ an hour. When cold add spice and ginger. Mix well, put into jars and cover when cold.

From Mrs. A. Johns, Flintshire.

BEET RELISH

1 quart cooked beetroot (which has been chopped fine).
1 quart chopped uncooked cabbage.
1 cupful freshly-grated horse-radish.
¼ lb. sugar.

Pinch of cayenne.
1 saltspoonful white pepper.
1 tablespoonful mustard.
1 teaspoonful salt.
1 pint vinegar.

MIX the ingredients well together and cook for ½ hour. Put into jars and cover closely. This is very good served with fish.

Mrs. H. Handy, Arthingworth Lodge, Market Harborough.

APPLE PICKLE

TAKE 6 lbs. of good cooking apples (Bramley Seedlings), peel, cut up into ¾-in. cubes, spread on dish and strew with a little salt; stand for 24 hours then drain. Put into a saucepan 3 pints of vinegar, 12 shallots cut up, ¾ lb. of lump sugar, 1 oz. of turmeric, ½ oz. ground ginger, ½ oz. mustard, 1 doz. cloves and peppercorns, the last two tied in muslin. Boil for 10 minutes, remove muslin bag, then add the strained apple chunks and cook for 15 minutes or until tender, without smashing.

From Mrs. W. J. Ford, Lower Farm, Cowhill, near Thornbury, Glos.

ORANGE PICKLE

6 oranges.
3 cupfuls white sugar.
2 cupfuls white vinegar.

1 teaspoonful each of cloves, cinnamon, lemon peel and mace all tied up in a muslin bag.

PEEL the oranges, cut into thick slices, remove pith and pips, then steam in a double saucepan, till clear and tender. Boil the sugar, vinegar and spices for ½ hour. Take out the muslin bag. Add the fruit and simmer very gently for 1 hour. Bottle in the usual way. This is delicious with cheese.

From Mrs. C. Gibbons, Three Chimneys, Poynton, Cheshire.

PICKLED ONIONS

2 quarts onions.
½ cupful sugar.
½ cupful salt.

½ packet mixed allspice.
Cloves and peppercorns.
1 quart pure malt vinegar.

PEEL the onions and place in a basin; sprinkle with salt. Stand overnight. Rinse well and dry. Boil the sugar, spices and vinegar for 5 minutes. Throw in the onions and boil up. Pack in bottles or jars and pour vinegar to overflowing. When cold cover closely.

From Miss C. M. Jones, Penlanwnws, Bwlchllan, Lampeter.

PICKLED MUSHROOMS

USE best vinegar and small button mushrooms. Prepare them by rubbing with a damp flannel dipped in salt. Put the mushrooms, sprinkled with a little salt and cayenne pepper, in a saucepan by the side of the fire. As the moisture runs out of them be careful they do not burn ; and when the moisture has been reabsorbed, cover them with vinegar. Leave them to simmer, but do not boil. Put them into jars and tie down when cold. *From Mrs. W. Roberts, The Lineare, Carlton, near Nuneaton.*

DAMSON PICKLE

4 lbs. damsons.
3 lbs. Demerara sugar.
½ pint vinegar.

¼ oz. cinnamon.
¼ oz. cloves.

BOIL sugar, cinnamon and cloves in vinegar for 10 minutes ; take out spices (which should be in muslin bag), and add fruit. Boil for 10 minutes, being careful not to break fruit when stirring. Put all into a large jar and tie down when cold. Prepared in this way, they will keep for years, and improve with keeping. Splendid with cold meat. Plums may be prepared the same way.

From Mrs. E. F. Crick, The Bridge Farm, Tannington, Suffolk.

PICKLED GREEN CABBAGE
A New Zealand Maori Dish

CUT up finely 1 large cabbage and 4 large onions, sprinkle with salt and allow to stand for 24 hours. Drain well through a colander or sieve, and then boil slowly in 1 quart of vinegar for 20 minutes.

Mix together 1 cupful of plain flour, 2 cupfuls of sugar, 2 teaspoonfuls of curry powder, and 2 tablespoonfuls of mustard in 1 pint of vinegar. Pour over the cabbage and boil all together for another 5 minutes. Bottle while hot, leave till cold, then cover and tie down in the usual way.

From Mrs. V. Cantwell, Rotherbank, Liss, Hants.

PICKLED PLUMS

USE firm, not quite ripe, plums if possible. Take 6 lbs. of plums, stick a clove in one end and a piece of cinnamon in the other end. Put them in the jar in which they are to be cooked. Add 3 lbs. of Demerara sugar and 1 pint of best vinegar. Put the cover on the jar and stand in the oven until it reaches boiling point. Take out the jar and leave until next day. Draw off liquid, boil it gently for ½ hour, pour it over the plums. Tie down when cold. This pickle keeps well.

From Mrs. A. M. Duckett, Keinton-Mandeville, Taunton, Somerset.

APPLE AND TOMATO CHUTNEY

1 lb. apples, cut small.
1 lb. onions (chopped).
1 lb. ripe tomatoes, skinned and sliced.
½ pint vinegar.

½ lb. very dark brown sugar.
1d. packet mixed pickling spice, tied in muslin (taken out after).
¼ lb. sultanas, ¼ lb. mustard seeds if liked.

SIMMER about 4 hours. *From Mrs. M. E. Lenton, Huntingdonshire.*

RIPE TOMATO CHUTNEY

8 lbs. ripe tomatoes.
1 lb. onions.
3 ozs. salt.
½ oz. cloves.

Cayenne pepper and ground ginger to taste, about ¾ teaspoonful of each.

BOIL for 2 hours, then heat through a sieve until nothing remains but the seeds, skin, etc. Return to pan, add 1 pint vinegar and 6 ozs. sugar, boil for ½ hour or until thick. This is appetising with fish, hot or cold, or with other meat dishes.

From Miss E. Henton, Windy Harbour Farm, Warton, Preston, Lancs.

INDIAN CHUTNEY

TAKE 3 lbs. apples, peeled and quartered, 2 large onions, finely chopped; boil to a pulp, in 1 quart of malt vinegar. Add 2 lbs. Barbados sugar; 1 lb. raisins, stoned and chopped; ½ lb. crystallized ginger, cut up very fine; 1 eggspoonful red pepper, 1 dessertspoonful dry mustard, 1 teaspoonful salt. Mix well together. Boil again for ½ hour, stirring often; then put into jars, and cover down. A little of this, added to meat stews or hashes before dishing up, is delicious. It also makes welcome Christmas presents if put in small fancy jars.

From Miss Westcott, Burnicombe Farm, Dunsford, near Exeter.

SPICED CARROTS

BOIL together ½ pint vinegar, ½ pint water, a few cloves, a little cinnamon, and salt to taste. Prepare about 12 medium-sized boiled carrots. Place in jars, allow the spiced vinegar to become cold, then pour over the carrots and tie down. Ready for use in a fortnight.

From Mrs. C. Gibbons, Three Chimneys, Poynton, Cheshire.

BENGAL CHUTNEY

1 lb. Demerara sugar.	½ lb. stoned raisins.
½ tablespoonful salt.	3 pints vinegar.
2 ozs. mustard seed.	¼ lb. garlic.
2 ozs. ground ginger.	¼ lb. onions.
½ oz. cayenne pepper.	15 large sour apples.

BAKE apples down to a pulp, and boil onions until tender in a little water. Bring the garlic to the boil, skim; then, with the raisins, put all the ingredients into a preserving pan and boil for ¼ hour. Put into jars and seal down. This chutney will keep for 2 or 3 years and improves with keeping.

From Miss M. C. Wood, Oxfordshire

GREEN TOMATO CHUTNEY

3 lbs. green tomatoes.	2 tablespoonfuls mustard.
4 large apples.	1½ teaspoonfuls ground ginger.
2 small cucumbers.	½ level teaspoonful cayenne.
3 large onions.	1½ tablespoonfuls salt.
6 ozs. sultanas.	4½ gills vinegar.
¾ lb. Demerara sugar.	

REMOVE stalks from tomatoes. Slice and peel onions and apples, slice cucumbers and put all the ingredients into a large pan. Bring to boil. Allow to simmer for 2 to 3 hours, or until quite soft, stirring frequently. Put into jars and seal down.

From Mrs. H. Nelson, Pembrokeshire.

DATE AND BANANA CHUTNEY

TWELVE bananas cut in slices, 2 lbs. onions cut small, 1 lb. dates chopped. Pour over about 1 pint vinegar and cook until tender. Beat to a pulp, add 2 teaspoonfuls of curry powder, ½ lb. crystallized ginger cut small, 1 tablespoonful salt and 1 lb. treacle. Cook again until a rich brown colour. This is a delicious chutney and can be made at any time.

From Mrs. H. Bampkin, Northampton.

MARROW CHUTNEY

4 lbs. marrow.	9 chillies.
½ lb. pickling onions.	1½ ozs. ground ginger.
6 cloves.	1½ ozs. mustard.
1½ lbs. loaf sugar.	2 pints vinegar.
½ oz. turmeric.	Salt.

CUT the marrow into small squares (about ½ in.), lay on a dish and shake some salt over it, leaving overnight. Now drain. Boil the other ingredients for 10 minutes, then add the marrow and boil for $\frac{1}{2}$ an hour, or until tender, and put into jars.   *From Mrs. T. Metcalfe, Yorkshire.*

ORANGE CHUTNEY

4 oranges : 2 apples.	$\frac{1}{2}$ oz. chopped chillies.
$\frac{1}{2}$ lb. brown sugar.	1 pint malt vinegar.
4 ozs. raisins.	1 oz. salt : a little pepper.
4 ozs. preserved ginger.	1 onion.

PEEL the oranges, remove pips and pith and cut into small pieces. Peel, core and chop apples finely. Chop the onion. Put these into a pan with the other ingredients and boil slowly until the fruit is tender (about 1 hour). Bottle and cover hot.

From Mrs. S. Allen, The Cottage, Tur Langton, Leicester.

TURNIP CHUTNEY

2 lbs. turnips.	$\frac{1}{2}$ oz. turmeric powder.
1 lb. apples.	1 teaspoonful mustard.
1 lb. onions.	$\frac{1}{4}$ teaspoonful pepper.
$\frac{1}{2}$ lb. sultanas.	2 ozs. salt.
$\frac{1}{2}$ lb. moist sugar.	1 quart brown vinegar.

CUT up the turnips and boil until soft. Drain out the water, beat to a pulp. Prepare the apples and onions, chopping them finely. Mix the turmeric powder and the mustard together, with a little vinegar. Put all the ingredients into the pan and boil for 1 hour. Stir. Put into jars and cover when cold.

From Mrs. Robinson, Staffordshire.

MANGOLD CHUTNEY

4 lbs. mangolds.	3 pints spiced vinegar.
1 lb. shallots.	Small tablespoonful turmeric.
$\frac{3}{4}$ lb. sugar.	

TAKE the mangolds, cut up and put through the mincer, using the largest knife. Sprinkle well with salt. Leave until next day. Then strain and add shallots, minced fine, sugar and vinegar. Boil altogether for about 1 hour. Just before taking off, put in the turmeric. This quantity makes 8 lbs. of chutney.

From Miss Hawkins, Berkshire.

DELICIOUS SWEET CHUTNEY

1 lb. dates, stoned and chopped.	2 ozs. ground ginger.
3 lbs. apples.	Pinch cayenne pepper.
1 quart vinegar.	A few cloves.
1 lb. onions.	

BOIL together for 1 hour and bottle when cold.

From Mrs. L. E. Long, Hampshire.

GOVERNOR'S SAUCE

12 lbs. green tomatoes.
12 large onions.
2 handfuls salt.
1 lb. brown sugar.
4 teaspoonfuls red pepper (if liked).

1½ teaspoonfuls ground white pepper.
1½ teaspoonfuls mustard.
Vinegar to cover the whole.
In a small muslin bag put 2 teaspoonfuls each of cloves, whole pepper and ginger.

WASH and cut tomatoes, peel onions and cut in slices, sprinkle over them the salt. Mix altogether and let stand all night. In the morning drain off the water and put fruit in preserving-pan (not copper), add vinegar, etc., and boil until soft. Remove muslin bag and put sauce in jars for use.

From Mrs. G. E. Jones, Lower House Farm, East Meon, Petersfield, Hants.

RHUBARB SAUCE

3 lbs. rhubarb.
¾ pint vinegar.
1 lb. sugar.
¼ lb. onions.
1 oz. salt.

Pinch cayenne pepper.
3 teaspoonfuls turmeric.
2 teaspoonfuls mustard.
6 cloves.

PEEL and cut rhubarb as for stewing ; peel onions and cut up, put into pan with a little of the vinegar, salt, cloves and pepper ; boil gently about 1 hour. Pass mixture through a sieve, return to pan, add remains of vinegar and sugar, bring to boil and add turmeric and mustard, mixed with a little vinegar to a smooth paste. Boil gently about ¾ to 1 hour, till thick ; cool a little and bottle and cork tightly.

From Mrs. L. J. Feltham, Cherry Hill, Painswick, Stroud, Glos.

HAW SAUCE

1½ lbs. haws.
4 ozs. sugar.
1 oz. salt.

3 gills vinegar.
½ teaspoonful white pepper.

GATHER the haws and wash them well. Put into an enamel pan with the vinegar and cook over a gentle heat for 30 minutes ; then press through a sieve ; return to the pan with sugar, salt and pepper, and boil for 10 minutes. Pour into pots and seal. This sauce keeps splendidly.

From Miss E. Rutherford, Tweedmouth.

A SAUCE FOR COLD MEAT

SLICE 6 smooth-skinned lemons, rub 3 ozs. salt into them, after removing the pips. Mix together 2 ozs. each of allspice, mustard seed, white pepper and horseradish, and 1 oz. each of mace, cayenne and cloves. Put the lemon slices in layers in a jar. Sprinkle the mixed spices between, and pour over them 2 quarts vinegar at boiling point. Set aside for 24 hours: squeeze, strain and bottle.

From Miss H. West, Halden View, Bridford, Exeter.

HOT SAUCE

¼ lb. garlic.
¼ lb. mixed spice.
1 teaspoonful celery seeds.
1 stick cinnamon.
¼ lb. horseradish.

1 small bottle Indian soy.
Vinegar.
Onion pickle vinegar.
Walnut pickle vinegar.

PUT garlic and horseradish through mincer. Boil all spices in good vinegar, and when cold pour over garlic and horseradish and celery seeds. Keep in a large pickling bottle and shake every day. Add the vinegar from walnut and onion pickles, also the soy.

From Miss Standen, Cheswick House, Huntingdon.

NASTURTIUM SAUCE

1 quart pressed nasturtium flowers.
1 quart vinegar
8 shallots, well bruised.
6 cloves.

1 teaspoonful salt
½ level teaspoonful cayenne pepper.
A little Indian soy.

SIMMER all except the flowers together for 10 minutes, then pour over the flowers. Cover closely for 2 months. Strain, and pour into bottles, adding a little Indian soy before corking securely.

From Mrs. F. S. Ashford, Wiltshire.

PICKLED PEARS

7 lbs. (stewing or hard) pears.
3½ lbs. lump sugar.
1 large lemon.

½ pint white vinegar.
½ oz. root ginger (bruised).
A few cloves.

BOIL ingredients together for 2 minutes, add pears (peeled and halved—if placed in cold water as soon as peeled they will keep white). Boil until tender. It is advisable to keep a cover on the stewing pan to keep in all steam until sufficent liquid covers the pears. Turn into dry bottles and tie down securely.

From Mrs. Arthur Lea, Cornwall.

SALAD DRESSING

2 pints milk.
4 dessertspoonfuls mustard.
2 tablespoonfuls flour.
2 dessertspoonfuls salt.
4 tablespoonfuls sugar.

1 teaspoonful pepper.
1 pint vinegar.
2 eggs.
2 tablespoonfuls salad oil.

MIX together flour, sugar, salt, pepper, mustard and oil. Well beat the eggs, add milk, and stir gradually into the other ingredients. Lastly add vinegar, drop by drop. Pour into the saucepan, and stir over fire until simmering. Simmer for 5 minutes. Use double saucepan to prevent burning.

From Mrs. S. Yates, Buckinghamshire.

SALAD CREAM

1 tablespoonful mustard.
1 tablespoonful sugar.
1 teaspoonful flour.
½ teaspoonful salt.

2 eggs.
¾ breakfastcupful vinegar.
Cream.

MIX mustard, sugar, flour and salt together; add the eggs, then vinegar. Stand in boiling water and stir until mixture thickens. Allow it to get quite cold, then add cream (and a little milk, if necessary) till mixture is the required thickness. This salad cream will keep 12 months.

From Mrs. G. R. Smith, Gate House, Lower Bentham, near Lancaster.

MAYONNAISE

MIX together 1 dessertspoonful flour, 1 tablespoonful castor sugar, 1 teaspoonful dry mustard, 1 teaspoonful salt, and a dash of pepper. Break in 2 eggs, beat thoroughly with a spoon, then stir in gradually a breakfastcupful of milk and a teacupful of vinegar, adding them alternately. When all is blended, stir over a gentle heat until it thickens, then beat in 2 oz. fresh butter.

From Mrs. D. M. Mann, Kings Ash Farm, The Lee, Great Missenden.

HOME-MADE HOT SAUCE

1 pint vinegar.
2 tablespoonfuls flour.
3 tablespoonfuls sugar.
1 teaspoonful salt.

2 tablespoonfuls treacle.
1 tablespoonful mustard.
1 pennyworth pickling spice.

MIX all together and boil for 20 minutes, then put through a strainer. When cold, bottle and cork. This is very tasty.

From Miss Dilys Morgan, Flintshire.

PRESERVES

HOME-MADE PECTIN

APPLES contain a large amount of pectin and those housewives who are fortunate enough to have a good crop would perhaps like to try the following recipe.

Choose apples of the soft kind which " fall " when cooked. Prepare as for jelly making and when cooking barely cover the apples with water. Strain through a coarse jelly bag, but do not squeeze. Several lots can be prepared in this way and bottled in one operation. Heat to actual boiling point and have ready screw-topped bottles of the Kilner type which must also have been heated to prevent cracking when the liquid is poured in. Screw down at once as in fruit bottling and store away until next summer, and when using allow to every tumblerful of pectin $\frac{3}{4}$ lb. sugar.

A slight cloudiness need not cause anxiety as this automatically disappears in the process of jam or jelly making. Strawberry jam to which this apple pectin is added has a delightful flavour and sets beautifully, as also do the other fruits which contain very little natural pectin.

From L. Watson, Earls Barton, Northampton.

APPLE PRESERVE

| Apples. | Water. |
| 1 lb. preserving sugar to each pint of juice and pulp. | 1 lemon to every 2 pints. |

WIPE the apples, no matter how small provided they are perfectly sound ; pare and core and slice them as for a stew. Put the pieces into a preserving-pan, adding sufficient water to keep them from sticking. Cook until quite tender, take out the pulp and place in a bowl.

Put all the cores and peel and thinly pared lemon rind into the preserving-pan with sufficient water to cover, stirring occasionally; cook until tender. Then put into a muslin strainer or jelly-bag and leave for 24 hours.

Next day take the apple pulp and the liquid. Boil together, and to every pint add 1 lb. preserving sugar and the strained lemon juice. Boil the whole quickly until it coats the back of the wooden spoon with which it is stirred. Put into small moulds or jars and tie down, when cold, in the usual way. It is delicious for tea, or with roast pork, and makes a pleasant addition to a crust of bread and cheese.

From Mrs. Frank Carding, Cars Banks, Farnsfield, Notts.

APPLE GINGER

4 lbs. apples.   4 lbs. granulated sugar.
3 pints water.   2 ozs. ground ginger.

GOOD for using up apples that do not keep well. Golden russets make a beautiful-looking preserve of a golden red hue, equally popular at tea-time or for filling tarts, or dumplings. Make a thick syrup of the sugar and water by boiling together. Peel, core and cut apples into thin slices and boil in the syrup until transparent, then add ginger, boil for another 5 minutes. Bottle and seal.

From Mrs. L. Fox, Norfolk.

APPLE JELLY
(*Clove flavoured*)

THE tiny rosy-cheeked apples will do for this jelly. Put apples in jelly-pan, and barely cover with water: boil till pulpy. Then strain all night through a jelly bag. To every pint of juice add 1 lb. preserving sugar and 2 cloves; tie the cloves in a piece of muslin and lift out when jelly is ready. It takes about ½ hour boiling rapidly. Test on cold plate, then pot. This is a tinted and delicious jelly.

From Mrs. Wright, North Belton, Dunbar, East Lothian.

APPLE AND APRICOT JAM

1 lb. dried apricots.   Sugar.
12 lbs. windfall apples.   Water.

CUT apricots in small pieces, soaking thoroughly in 1 pint of water, or as much as they will absorb. Wash and cut up apples without peeling. Boil till soft in enough water to ensure thorough cooking. Then strain, squeezing through all the pulp. Add apricots, weigh, and bring to the boil. To each pound of pulp allow ¾ lb. of sugar (or 1 lb. to 1 pint). Boil fast till it sets when tested. Stir well. The faster it boils the deeper the colour, and stronger the flavouring of the jam.

From Mrs. Daniels, Bedfordshire.

APPLE AND PLUM CHEESE

3 lbs. apples.   ¾ lb. sugar to every pint of pulp.
1 lb. plums.

PEEL, core and slice apples ; and cook in a little water until nearly tender. Add plums, and cook until soft. Rub through a sieve, and boil up with the sugar. Directly it sets, pour into jars. This is a good way of using up windfall apples.

From Mrs. L. Tyler, Yorkshire.

APRICOT JAM

2 lbs. dried apricots.   3 quarts water.
6 lbs. preserving sugar.   1 oz. bitter almonds.

WASH the apricots quickly in warm water and then soak them in 3 quarts of fresh, cold water for 24 hours. Boil fast for ½ hour. Add the sugar and stir over a low fire until it has dissolved. Bring to the boil again and boil fast until it sets. Pour boiling water on to the almonds and rub off the skins. Put the almonds into the jam as soon as it has finished boiling. This makes about 12 lbs. of jam which is both good and cheap.

From Mrs. M. A. Armstrong, Sycamores, Rowley, Consett.

APRICOT CURD

½ lb. apricots.   ½ lb. castor sugar.
1 lemon.   Very little water.
2 ozs. butter.

WASH the fruit and put in a preserving-pan, or saucepan, with a very little water and cook until soft ; then pass them through a sieve. Put the fruit into a double saucepan, with the sugar, butter, the juice and grated rind of the lemon. When the sugar has dissolved, add the beaten eggs and stir mixture until it thickens. Pour into hot jars and cover.

From Mrs. E. A. Thomas, Broome Hall Farm, Coldharbour, Surrey.

BLACKBERRY AND ELDERBERRY JAM

TAKE equal quantities of blackberries and elderberries (stripped of the stalks), put in a preserving-pan, squeeze slightly, bring slowly to the boil and boil for 20 minutes. Allow ¾ lb. of sugar to each 1 lb. of fruit. Put sugar on a dish and place in the oven to get hot before adding it to the jam. Bring again to the boil and boil for 20 minutes. Cover while hot. This jam is cheap and will keep for 12 months.

From Miss F. McIntyre, Suffolk.

BLACK CURRANT JAM

3 lbs. sugar } To every 1½ lbs. of fruit.
1 pint of water

STALK and cut brown ends off fruit. Boil fruit and water together for 20 minutes, then add the sugar and boil for 5 minutes. Made in this way, the preserve will keep for 2 or 3 years.

From Mrs. Ford, Lower Farm, Cowhill, near Thornbury, Glos.

CARROT JAM

Carrots.   Lemon.
Sugar.   Sweet almonds.
Cooking brandy.

TO 1 pint of purée allow 1 lb. of sugar, 1 lemon, ½ oz. sweet almonds, and 1 tablespoonful cooking brandy.

Wash and clean carrots, and cut into small pieces. Cook until tender in as little water as possible, and rub through a sieve. Measure the purée, put it into a preserving-pan with the sugar, grated lemon rind and strained juice of the lemon. Stir until the sugar is melted, then boil until the jam will set. Add the almonds (blanched and shredded) and the brandy. This jam will not keep without the brandy.

From Miss P. Malin, Warwickshire.

PRESERVED CHERRIES

TAKE fine sugar, put a little water to it, and boil it. Stone your cherries, put them in the sugar, boil, and let them stand in the syrup 2 or 3 days. Boil the syrup again, pour it over the cherries, let them stand some time, then lay them on a sieve to dry. *From N. A. Robby, Cumberland.*

Preserves

CHESTNUT JAM

2 lbs. chestnuts.
1½ lbs. loaf sugar.

3 tablespoonfuls vanilla essence.
½ pint water to make the syrup.

BOIL the chestnuts until ready. Peel and skin them. Time can be saved both in boiling and peeling them if you first cut a cross on both sides of the chestnuts. They should boil for 20 minutes to ½ hour. Then crush through a wire sieve.

Make a syrup with ½ pint of water, sugar and essence. When it is ready put in the crushed chestnuts, and cook gently until fairly stiff. Put in hot glass jars and cover. Always store this jam in a dry place.

From Miss Alice Wakelin, Cambridge.

DAMSON JAM

4 lbs. damsons (ripe).
4 lbs. sugar.

¾ cup (small) of vinegar.
¾ cup of water.

PUT the vinegar, sugar and water into pan, and boil until it syrups; then put in ripe fruit and boil 10 minutes.

From Miss M. A. Hutchinson, Ayham Lodge, Kendal.

DAMSON CHEESE

PUT some sound ripe fruit into a stone jar (or casserole), cover it, and bake in a very cool oven until the damsons are tender. Then drain off the juice, skin and stone the fruit, and put it into a preserving-pan. Pour back on them from a third, to half, of their juice, and boil over a clear fire until they form a dry paste. Add fine sugar, in the proportion of 6 ozs. to each pound of the fruit. Then stir continuously over the fire until the sugar has dissolved, and the fruit comes away dry from the sides of the pan. Press it into small jars, or moulds, and when perfectly cold place on the top of each a round of paper that has been dipped in spirit. Fasten securely, and store in a dry place. Will keep for months.

From Miss E. Evans, Northamptonshire.

DAMSON AND APPLE JELLY

USING equal quantities of damsons and apples, add ½ pint of cold water to 1 lb. of fruit. Boil until fruit is quite soft. Strain through muslin; weigh the juice, and allow 1 lb.

sugar to 1 lb. of the liquid. Boil the juice quickly for 15 minutes, then add sugar and boil together for ½ hour. This jelly is perfectly clear, and will keep for 12 months at least.

From Mrs. M. F. Corfield, Montgomeryshire.

DATE JAM

STONE and cut into dice 6 lbs. dates, wash and clean 8 lbs. carrots and chop finely. Put dates and carrots into a preserving-pan with 6 lbs. sugar, 1 oz. blanched sweet almonds cut in halves, and 3 pints water. Boil mixture until it jellies and put in pots and tie down.

From Mrs. M. F. Palmer, Mill Farm, Snetterton, Warwick.

FIG AND LEMON PRESERVE

2 lbs. figs.
2 pints cold water.

4 lemons (rind and juice).
3 lbs. sugar.

WASH the figs, remove the stalks and cut into about 6 pieces. Put them into a basin with the water and leave soaking for 24 hours. Turn into a preserving pan, add sugar and cook slowly until dissolved, then bring to the boil and remove the scum. Wipe lemons and grate rind finely, squeeze out juice and strain it. Add both these to the figs and boil all together until it will jelly when cold, keeping it stirred and skimmed as required. Cool, pot and when cold, tie down.

From Mrs. W. A. Francy, Eastwood Poultry Farm, Barrow-on-Soar,
Leics.

GOOSEBERRY MINT JELLY

2 lb. green gooseberries.
½ doz. stalks fresh green mint.

Sugar.

WASH the gooseberries and put them in a preserving-pan ; nearly cover them with cold water, and cook until they are soft and pulpy. Strain the fruit through a sieve, being careful to extract all the juice. To each pint of liquid add 1 lb. of sugar, put in a preserving-pan with mint tied in a bundle. Boil gently until the jelly will set, stirring frequently. Remove the mint, pour the jelly into pots, and seal at once.

From Mrs. A. Jones, Flintshire.

HAW JELLY
(*Excellent with Cold Meat*)

GATHER 3 lbs. haws, wash them well and put into a pan with 3 pints of water; simmer for 1 hour, then pour into a jelly bag and leave to strain overnight. Next morning measure the juice and return to the pan with 1 lb. of sugar and the strained juice of 1 lemon to each pint of juice. Boil until the jelly will set when tested.

From Miss E. Rutherford, Tweedmouth.

MOCK LEMON CURD

1 lemon.	1 egg.
1 teacupful water.	1 teaspoonful cornflour.
1 teacupful granulated sugar.	A small piece butter or margarine.

GRATE lemon peel into saucepan with water, sugar and butter, boil gently a few minutes, thicken with the cornflour mixed with the lemon juice. Remove from the fire a few minutes and when off the boil mix in the well-beaten egg, but do not boil up again, or the egg will curdle. This is a nice change from jam.

From Mrs. F. H. Dancer, Buckinghamshire.

LEMON CHEESE

2 eggs.	8 ozs. sugar.
2 lemons.	5 ozs. butter.

PEEL the lemons as thinly as possible, and squeeze out the juice. Put both the rind and the juice in a saucepan with the sugar and butter and dissolve very slowly. Beat up the eggs, then stir the lemon, etc., on to them. Strain, return to the pan, and stir over a low burner until the mixture comes to the boil and is thick and creamy. The cheese may be made most satisfactorily in a double saucepan. The steaming ensures the slow melting of the sugar and butter which is so essential. I find this recipe most useful as a means of using up cracked eggs.

From Mrs. E. Beveridge, Fifeshire.

MARROW JAM

5½ lbs. marrow.   3 lemons.
5½ lbs. sugar.   ½ lb. crystallized ginger.
Salt.

CUT up the marrow; place in a bowl; sprinkle ¾ of a teacupful of salt; leave for 12 hours. Then strain off the salty water, and put the sugar on the marrow; allow to stand for 12 hours or longer. Add the lemons and the ginger cut small, and boil all together until the marrow is quite transparent.

From Mrs. H. W. Oglesby, E. Yorkshire.

MARROW CREAM

2 lbs. marrow.   ¼ lb. butter.
2 lbs. lump sugar.   2 lemons.

PEEL the marrow and boil until it is quite soft; strain well and beat to a pulp. Then put into a saucepan with the sugar, butter, and the juice and grated rind of the lemons. Boil slowly altogether for ¾ hour. This makes a filling equally as nice as lemon cheese.

From Mrs. S. Mills, Warwickshire.

MARROW AND PINEAPPLE JAM

PEEL a marrow, remove the seeds, cut into small pieces, weigh, and to each pound of marrow add ¾ lb. sugar. Put into a stone jar and leave overnight. Next day add the chunks—1 small tin to each 2 lb. marrow (without the syrup). Cut each chunk into 3 or 4 pieces. Boil for 2 hours or until the pine is soft and the jam sets. This is delicious for pastry tarts.

From Mrs. F. Steward, Suffolk.

JAM AND JELLY FROM FALLEN APPLES AND PLUMS

JAM

3 lbs. apples.   3 lbs. plums.
Lump sugar.

PEEL and core the apples (save the peels and cores for making the jelly). Stone the plums, and cook the apples and plums with 1½ pints of water until soft. Then add sugar, and boil fast until it will set when tried on a plate. This will take about 20 minutes. Skim and put into jars, and tie down when cold.

JELLY

Having saved the peels and cores of the apples, put them into a large saucepan and just cover with water, cooking until pulpy. Strain through a jelly bag ; and measure. To every pint of juice add 1 lb. of lump sugar, and boil fast until it sets. This jelly is equal to that made with whole apples.

From Miss N. Fennell, Warwickshire.

QUINCE JELLY

PARE and slice the quinces, and put in a preserving-pan with sufficient water to float them. Boil until fruit is reduced to a pulp. Strain the clear juice through a jelly bag, and to each pint allow 1 lb. loaf sugar. Boil juice and sugar together for about $\frac{3}{4}$ hour, removing all scum as it rises; and, when the jelly appears firm, pot up at once into small jars.

QUINCE JAM

(From the pulp left over from the preceding recipe)

Put the pulp through a sieve, or mash very finely with wooden spoon. Put $\frac{1}{2}$ lb. granulated sugar to each 1 lb. of pulp, and boil till it sets. Keep well stirred to prevent burning. Cover when cold.

From Miss H. Jenner, Kent.

RASPBERRY PRESERVE

4 lbs. raspberries.   5 lbs. sugar.

PLACE the raspberries on a large dish and put into a hot oven. Then place the sugar on another large dish and put that also into the oven. When they are very hot (not boiling), beat the fruit thoroughly, then gradually add the hot sugar, beating all well together until the sugar is dissolved. It is then ready to be put in the jars. This jam will keep any length of time, and has the flavour of freshly-gathered fruit. It is easily made, as there is no boiling or simmering.

From Mrs. B. A. Moor, Yorkshire.

POTTED RASPBERRIES

4 lbs. fine white sugar.   1 oz. fresh butter.
4 lbs. raspberries.

PICK over the berries, using also the bruised ones. Have sugar heated in a bowl in a warm oven. Rub butter round a preserving-pan, put over a very low gas, and place the berries in. When they start to bubble, pour into the warm sugar. Beat with a wooden spoon for 30 minutes and put into pots and cover.

This will make 8 lbs. of a lovely preserve with real raspberry flavour and colour. There is no waste, and it will keep indefinitely.   *From Mrs. J. A. Forbes, Co. Tyrone.*

RHUBARB CONSERVE

TAKE as much rhubarb as you wish, when it is tender and full grown. Cut off both ends of each stick, but do not peel it. Rub with a cloth and cut in pieces about 1 in. long. To each pound of rhubarb allow 1 lb. of sugar, and put alternately into a dish. Let it stand 24 hours, by which time the sugar should be in a liquid state. Pour the liquid in a pan and boil briskly for ½ hour, then add the rhubarb with crystallized ginger (about 2 ozs. to 1 lb. rhubarb, or more if liked), boil for another ½ hour. Take off the fire and let it stand for ½ hour before putting into pots.

From Miss E. T. Daltry, St. Roman, Single Street, Biggin Hill, Kent.

RHUBARB AND MINT JELLY
(*for serving with lamb*)

WIPE some rhubarb and cut into pieces. Stew until soft and pulpy, then strain through a fine sieve. To each pint of juice allow 1 lb. of loaf sugar. Put juice and sugar into a preserving-pan with some fresh clean mint tied into bundles.

Boil until the jelly thickens when tested on a cold plate, stirring often. Remove mint before pouring into small pots. Choose rhubarb that has pale pink stalks.

From Mrs. Foster, Rye Foreign, Peasmarsh, Sussex.

RHUBARB AND MIXED PEEL JAM
4 lbs. rhubarb.   ½ lb. mixed peel.
4 lbs. sugar.

WIPE the rhubarb without peeling, slice it the long way of the sticks, and cut into pieces about the size of a large pea. Put the rhubarb and sugar in layers with the mixed peel in a preserving-pan, and let it remain till the next day. Strain off the juice, and boil for ¼ hour. Then pour it over the fruit, covering the pan to keep in the steam. Next day boil jam quickly for about ½ hour, or till it jells. Many people who do not like rhubarb jam made in the usual way appreciate this recipe.   *From Miss V. Wadman, Wiltshire.*

RHUBARB AND ORANGE JAM

TO every pound of rhubarb, add 2 fair-sized apples and 2 sweet oranges, 4 ozs. sugar, ¼ teaspoonful each of mixed spice and ground ginger, ½ teaspoonful of salt. Bring slowly to the boil, then boil briskly for 20 minutes, or till the apples slices are clear.

From Mrs. E. Downes, Shropshire.

GREEN TOMATO JAM

4 lbs. tomatoes.   3 lbs. preserving sugar.
Flavouring.

BREAK up the tomatoes, put them into the preserving-pan, and let them come to the boil. Add the sugar, a few cloves, or a small piece of whole ginger, or the grated rind of a lemon for flavouring. Boil fast for 20 minutes. It will set when placed on a plate in a cool place. This is an excellent way of preserving outdoor tomatoes that do not ripen well.

From Mrs. Baker, Monmouthshire.

RED TOMATO JAM

SCALD the tomatoes and remove the skins. Cut into 4 pieces and put into a pan with the sugar, allowing ¾ lb. to each pound of tomatoes. Add the juice of 2 lemons to every 3 lbs. of fruit, and a small teaspoonful of ground ginger. Stir well with a wooden spoon. Boil gently for about 3 hours, skimming often until a little sets on being tested. Put into clean, warm jars, and when cold tie down.

From Mrs. Craig, Hatchwoods Cottage, Odiham, Hants.

EMERGENCY MARMALADE

8 sweet oranges.   10 pints water.
2 large grapefruits.   7 lbs. sugar.
2 lemons.

REMOVE the juice and pips from the fruit. Put the fruit through the mincer and soak with the juice and water for 48 hours. Tie up pips in muslin and add to the above. After soaking, boil until the fruit is tender (about 2 hours). Remove the bag of pips and add the sugar ; boil fast until marmalade jellies. This quantity makes about 15 lbs.

From Miss E. Lenton, Brampton, Hunts.

JELLIED MARMALADE

USE 1 sweet orange and 1 lemon to every 4 Seville oranges. Allow roughly 1 pint of water to every pound of fruit. Grate off only the yellow rinds of fruit. Remove all the white pith. Slice the pulp and put it into a preserving-pan with the water. Boil for ½ hour. Stir occasionally. Strain through a sieve (hair) or clean scalded cloth. Measure the liquid, and allow 1 lb. of best sugar to each pint. Put the juice and sugar into a pan. Add the grated rinds of fruit. Stir until the sugar has melted. Boil fast from 10 to 15 minutes or until the mixture jellies when tested. Keep skimmed. Put into small pots and cover.

From Mrs. Letitia Davies, Carmarthenshire.

APPLE AND GRAPEFRUIT MARMALADE

TAKE 3 grapefruits, cut into pieces. Put pips and cores into a basin and cover with boiling water. To each pound of grapefruit pulp add 1 pint of water and soak overnight. Next add same amount of apple juice as water (previously strained as for jelly), and bring to boil, adding ¾ lb. of sugar to each pint of liquid previously measured (grapefruit, water and apple juice together). Boil fast for about 1 hour (with the pips, etc., in muslin bag), when the marmalade should form a jelly when tested. Pour into warm jars, and seal with greaseproof paper while still hot. Pips boiled in the pan cause the jelly to form more quickly.

From Miss Geraldine Ward, Brook Farm, Alresford, Essex.

GRAPEFRUIT MARMALADE

3 lbs. grapefruit.   4½ pints water.
2 small lemons.   7½ lbs. sugar.

SLICE the grapefruit finely, place the lemon and grapefruit pips in 1 pint of boiling water and soak. Grate the rind of the lemons, peel them, throw away the pith of the rind. Add the grated rind and the inside of the lemons, finely chopped, to the grapefruit, and cover with the remaining 3½ pints of cold water. Stand for about 24 hours. Place in the preserving-pan with the water strained from the pips and simmer for ½ hour. Be very careful not to let it boil. Then add the sugar and bring to the boil. Boil rapidly for about 1 hour, or until it sets when tested. Pour into hot jars and tie down when cold.

From Mrs. E S. Willcocks, Clifton Farm, Landulph, Saltash, Cornwall.

PINEAPPLE MARMALADE

3 Jaffa oranges.
1 lemon.
1 large tin of pineapple.

4 lbs. sugar.
1 pint water.

WASH and peel both the lemon and oranges ; cut up the peel in thin shreds, and the fruit into small cubes ; cover with pineapple juice and 1 pint of water, leaving to soak all night. Then simmer gently in a preserving-pan until tender, add sugar and cook for ¾ hour, put in glass jars and seal when cool.

From Miss M. Cook, Twin Tree Farm, Neston Disney, Lincoln.

TOMATO MARMALADE

7 lbs. tomatoes.
8 lbs. loaf sugar.

½ pint water.
6 lemons.

SKIN tomatoes and cut in halves. Peel lemons and cut in slices. Put sugar and water in a pan. Stir gently till the sugar is dissolved. Skim and boil to a syrup. Add tomatoes and lemons and boil, stirring all the time. Remove scum as it rises. When the marmalade is sufficiently cooked it will hang in thick gelatinous flakes. When done, fill into jars and store.

From Mrs. Smith, Cote House Farm, Catterick.

" PUTTING-UP " APPLES

PARE, core and quarter a quantity of sound apples. Pack them tightly in wide-mouthed bottles. Add 1 lb. sugar and 1 small teaspoonful alum to 3 lbs. apples. Dissolve the sugar and alum in boiling water, cool and almost fill the bottles with it ; put these into a fish kettle. Set on the fire and cook very gently until the fruit looks soft. Fill the bottles up to the brim and cork tightly with well-fitting corks which have been dipped in mutton fat.

From Mrs. H. Rees, Crwys Farm, Three Crosses, Gowerton, Swansea.

GLACÉ GRAPES

½ lb. green grapes.
8 ozs. golden syrup.

1 cup Demerara sugar.
2 ozs. unsalted butter.

MELT butter in a pan, add golden syrup and sugar, then stir till boiling. Boil till a little tested in cold water hardens, then remove from heat. While the mixture is cooling, cut grapes from stem in clusters of 2 or 3 and suspend them on a string. Dip in one cluster at a time in the mixture, and hang up on string to set. Serve on a glass dish lined with leaves.

From Mrs. C. Gibbons, Three Chimneys, Poynton.

CANDIED PEEL

TAKE 8 oranges or 8 lemons or 4 of each and wash them. Cut the lemons lengthwise and the oranges crosswise. Remove all pulp. Dissolve ½ oz. bi-carbonate of soda in a little hot water and pour it over the pieces of peel; then add sufficient boiling water to cover the peel entirely. Allow to stand for 20 minutes then rinse the peel in several waters. Cover the peel with cold water; bring to the boil and simmer until tender. Make a syrup of 1 lb. of sugar with ¾ of a pint of water; pour it over the peel and stand for 2 days. Draw off the syrup and add to it another ½ lb. sugar. Bring to the boil and simmer the peel in it until it looks clear. Take out the peel and dry it in a cool oven. Reduce the syrup by boiling it for about ½ hour. Dip the peel in it and once more dry in a cool oven. The syrup left over may be beaten up until it is cloudy and thick and then a little may be poured into each cup-shaped piece of candied peel.

From Mrs. E. Anderson, Home Farm Cottage, Leigh, Tonbridge.

CANDIED TOMATOES

| 4 lbs. yellow tomatoes. | 1 lb. loaf sugar. |
| 2 lemons | 1 pint water. |

POUR boiling water over the tomatoes, then peel them. Boil the sugar in a pint of water. Remove any scum, slice the lemons and add them. Then put in the tomatoes and simmer slowly until they look clear. Take out with a slice and put on a sieve. Boil the syrup until quite thick, then put the tomatoes in again. Simmer slowly for about 1 hour, then take out on the sieve again. Repeat once more, then flatten the tomatoes with a wooden spoon and dry in a warm oven. When dry put in glass jars. *From Miss D. Jeans, Drumwalt, Kirby Bellars, Melton Mowbray.*

PRESERVING PLUMS AS PRUNES

GET a shallow wooden box and stack the plums close together, stalks uppermost. Cover with a sheet of kitchen paper. Place on a rack above the stove for 18 hours; and afterwards at every opportunity when the oven is not required, allow it to cool and then place the box of plums in it, and leave the door open. As they shrink, place the plums closer together in the box.

When sufficiently dried, which will take 3 days, pack in airtight jars and store in a dry cupboard. If the box is place in a hot airing cupboard, the final drying can be more quickly accomplished. *From Mrs. A. Shute, Wootton Fitzpaine, Dorset.*

SWEETMEATS

TOFFEE

1 lb. Demerara sugar.	2 pinches flour.
½ lb. butter.	2 dessertspoonfuls treacle.

BOIL well for about 20 minutes till it will set in water. Put in a buttered flat tin in a cool place till cold, then break into pieces and tin.

From Mrs. Norris, Mareham Hill Farm, Horncastle.

LEMON AND ACID DROPS

1½ lbs. loaf sugar.	½ teaspoonful cream of tartar.
½ pint water.	

BOIL the loaf sugar, water and cream of tartar until the mixture acquires a pale yellow tinge. Add the essence of lemon to taste, and turn the preparation on to an oiled slab. Sprinkle on 1 dessertspoonful of tartaric acid ; work it well in, and, as soon as it is cool enough to handle, form into thin rolls. Cut off short pieces with the scissors, and roll into shape under the hand. Coat with sifted sugar, dry well and afterwards store in an airtight tin.

From Miss Eileen Porter, Welby Lodge, near Grantham, Lincs.

COCO-NUT ICE (1)

3 lbs. loaf sugar.	½ pint milk.
1 lb. desiccated coconut.	

PUT sugar and milk in saucepan, bring to the boil, have all sugar dissolved, boil 3 minutes. Take off the fire, and stir in the coco-nut. Let one-half remain white and colour remainder with a few drops of cochineal. A baking-tin is best to put it in to cool. Line tin with buttered paper. When cold cut in squares.

From Miss E. J. Brake, Gloucestershire.

COCO-NUT ICE (2)

1 lb. castor sugar.   1 teacupful milk.
¾ lb. coco-nut.   1 saltspoonful cream of tartar.

PUT sugar, milk and cream of tartar into a saucepan, and let
it come to the boil slowly. Boil 20 minutes, then stir in the
coco-nut. Rinse the mould out with cold water, then put half
the mixture into it, add a few drops of cochineal to the remainder
to colour it, place this with the other in the mould. When cold
it will turn out quite firm.

From Mrs. B. Tween, Essex.

RICE AND NUT CANDIES

MIX equal quantites of boiled rice, and skinned and chopped
nuts—walnuts, hazelnuts and almonds. Press into small
balls, about the size of marbles. Drop them into boiling syrup,
and then allow to cool and harden. The syrup is made by
boiling 1 lb. loaf sugar with 3 gills water, and a good pinch of
cream of tartar in the crock. It is then ready for dipping the
sweets.

From Mrs. C. Gibbons, Three Chimneys, Poynton, Stockport.

MARZIPAN POTATOES

MIX together 4 ozs. of sweet ground almonds, and 8 ozs. of
castor sugar with the whisked white of an egg and a few
drops of vanilla essence until a stiff paste is formed. Take small
quantities and shape into little " potatoes," then roll them in
cocoa to make them brown. They can be varied by placing a
small piece of sponge cake and just a little raspberry jam in the
centre with the marzipan rolled around.

From Miss I. Turner, Easton Farm, Pylle, Shepton Mallet, Somerset.

FUDGE

1 large tin of sweetened condensed   1 lb. Demerara sugar.
  milk.   ¼ lb. butter.

PLACE ingredients in a saucepan and cook until the mixture
candies, then beat well after lifting from the fire. Pour into
a well-buttered tin ; and when cool, cut into squares.

This fudge is good plain, but chocolate, walnuts or vanilla
flavouring may be added if preferred.

From Mrs. M. Peeling, Surrey.

COFFEE NUT FUDGE

2 cupfuls granulated sugar.   1 cupful clear strong coffee.
1 teaspoonful butter.   1 cupful chopped walnuts.

BOIL sugar, coffee and butter to a soft ball. Take from the fire, and beat to a cream. Stir in the nuts, pour into a greased tin, and cut into bars when cold.

From Miss Elizabeth Tudor, Cheshire.

WALNUT FUDGE

1 lb. brown sugar.   ½ teaspoonful vanilla essence.
½ pint thin cream.   ¼ lb. chopped walnuts.
1 tablespoonful syrup.

PUT the sugar, cream and syrup into a saucepan. Stir well until it comes to the boil, then boil for 15 to 20 minutes. Remove from fire, stir in walnuts and vanilla, place saucepan in a pan of cold water, and stir quickly until toffee becomes thick. Pour into a buttered tin, mark into squares with a knife, and leave till cold.

From Miss Muriel Broad, Cheshire.

DIVINITY FUDGE

2 cups white sugar,   1 cup corn syrup.
½ cup water.   2 rings chopped candied pine-
1 egg white.   apple.
⅓ cup candied cherries.   1 teaspoonful vanilla.

COOK the sugar, syrup and water till it forms a firm ball when dropped in cold water. Add the syrup to the beaten egg white, pouring slowly and beating constantly. When it begins to thicken, add flavouring and fruit. It may be dropped in spoonfuls on a buttered sheet or poured into a buttered pan and cut into squares.

CHOCOLATE FUDGE

2 cups white sugar.   2 squares unsweetened chocolate
½ cup corn syrup.   (or tablespoonfuls cocoa).
½ cup milk.

COOK all together until it forms a soft ball when dropped in cold water. Then add 1 tablespoonful butter, 1 tablespoonful vanilla extract, 1 cupful chopped walnuts and a pinch of salt. Remove from the heat and beat well. Pour into a buttered pan and mark into squares.

Both these recipes from Mrs. L. Morrow, R.R.2 Sardis, British Columbia,
Canada.

COTTAGE CANDY

1 lb. brown sugar.
1 tablespoonful (heaped) butter.

4 tablespoonfuls milk (tinned milk is splendid).

BOIL all together till the mixture thickens ; remove from heat, and beat hard till creamy. Cool in buttered tray ; and mark into squares while warm. Chopped dates, nuts, crystallized fruits, may be added for variety.

From Mrs. M. Wilson, The Outpost, Edgehill, Ponteland,
Northumberland.

WALNUT TABLET

2 lbs. brown sugar.
1 cupful milk (creamy if possible).
1 tablespoonful syrup.

About 1½ ozs. butter.
About 2 ozs. shelled walnuts.
Vanilla.

PUT sugar, milk, syrup and butter in a pan. Stir over fire till it melts, then boil fairly hard for about 10 minutes. If, when tested in water, it is fairly firm, add vanilla to taste, then chopped walnuts. Remove from fire and beat till it " sugars." Pour at once into well-greased tin and when partly cooled mark in squares which can be easily separated when cold.

From Mrs. R. Weir, Ladyflat, Duns, Berwick.

CHOCOLATE TRUFFLES

One 4 oz. block plain chocolate.
2 ozs. icing sugar.
½ teaspoonful vanilla essence.

1½ tablespoonfuls unsweetened evaporated milk.
Desiccated coconut.

MELT the chocolate, but do not allow to get hot, stir in the sieved icing sugar and add the milk. Now add vanilla essence and work all together well. No cooking is needed. Shape into balls, then roll in the coconut.

From Mrs. Rogers, Acton Park, Wrexham.

APRICOT JUJUBES

1 lb. dried apricots : 2¼ lbs. granulated sugar.   Icing sugar : minced nuts.

SOAK the apricots for 24 hours. Put through a mincing machine twice. They should now weigh 2 lbs., but water may be added to make up the weight if necessary. Put the apricots and the granulated sugar together in a preserving-pan and cook over a gentle flame for 1 hour, stirring frequently to prevent sticking. Pour into shallow moulds or on to plates, and leave to cool. When sufficiently cool, it should cut cleanly with a knife that has been dipped in icing sugar. Roll the pieces in the minced nuts and icing sugar.

From Miss D. Hemus, Arundels Farm, Wichenford, near Worcester.

PEPPERMINT JELLIES

SOAK 1 oz. leaf gelatine in ½ teacupful of cold water for 2 hours ; or, better still, all night. Boil 1 lb. granulated sugar in ½ teacupful of cold water. When thoroughly boiling add soaked gelatine and stir until all are well mixed. Boil slowly for 20 minutes, watching the mixture carefully, as it quickly boils over. Then add ½ teaspoonful essence of peppermint and a few drops of green colouring. Stand a sandwich-tin in cold water for a few minutes, pour mixture into wet tin, then put away till next day. Turn out on to a sheet of paper covered with icing sugar, cut up into neat squares with scissors, and coat well with icing sugar.

This makes about 1½ lbs. of delicious sweets at a small cost. The flavouring and colouring may be varied.

From Mrs. E. A. Thomas, Broome Hall Farm, Coldharbour, Dorking.

CANADIAN PENOCHI

PUT together in a saucepan 3 cupfuls of light brown sugar, 1 small cupful of milk, and 2 tablespoonfuls of butter. Bring the mixture to the boil, stirring all the time with a wooden spoon, then allow it to boil with an occasional stir for 5 minutes. Add 1 cupful of either chopped walnuts, almonds, peanuts or a mixture of desiccated coco-nut and chopped preserved ginger. Boil, stirring constantly, until a little dropped in cold water forms a soft ball. Then add 1 teaspoonful of vanilla essence. Remove the pan from fire, and beat until the mixture is creamy. Pour into a butter-tin and cut into cubes when almost cold.

A delicious variation of this can be made by substituting granulated sugar for the brown, and chopped pineapple (well drained) for the nuts. Essence of lemon should be substituted for the vanilla in this case.

From Miss M. Turner, Loves Farm, Easebourne, Midhurst, Sussex.

CHRISTMAS FARE

PLUM PUDDING

TAKE 1½ lbs. each of potatoes and carrots boiled and weighed when cold ; rub through a colander, or put through a mincing machine ; 1½ lbs. each of raisins, currants, flour and suet, 1 lb. moist brown sugar, 1 small nutmeg, ½ lb. candied peel, 1 lemon (juice and grated rind), 6 tablespoonsful of treacle. Mix together and boil 6 hours. Boil for another 4 hours before using.

From Mrs. J. Band, Althorne, Essex.

CHRISTMAS PUDDING USING CARROTS AND OLD ALE

7 ozs. flour.	7 ozs. breadcrumbs.
14 ozs. beef suet.	½ lb. mixed peel.
14 ozs. currants.	10 ozs. sultanas.
½ lb. Demerara sugar.	1 oz. ground almonds.
½ lemon.	⅛ teaspoonful grated nutmeg.
3 eggs.	¼ lb. carrots.
1 gill old ale.	¼ teaspoonful ground cinnamon.
½ lb. stoned raisins.	⅛ teaspoonful mixed spice.
⅛ oz. baking powder.	Silver pudding favours.

PREPARE suet, currants, peel, raisins and sultanas as for mincemeat. Sift flour with salt, spices, and baking powder into a large mixing bowl. Rub crumbs through a wire sieve. Scrape, wash and dry carrots, then grate them. Turn into basin containing fruit and suet. Stir crumbs and sugar into flour mixture. Add suet and fruit and mix well. Stir in washed, dried and grated lemon rind. Cover basin with a clean cloth and stand overnight in a cool but dry place. Next day stir in the ale and strained lemon juice with your hand, and keep mixing until well incorporated. Beat eggs well together in a basin, and stir in with your hand. If eggs are small you may need 2 more, or add a little more ale. Beat well, then bury the pudding favours in the mixture.

Fill buttered basins or moulds with the mixture, but only to within 1 in. of the top, to allow for swelling. Cover with buttered paper, tie securely, then tie up with pudding cloths. Steam for 7 hours. Store in a dry but airy cupboard till required, then put to steam for another 2 hours. The quantities given will make 2 large puddings.

From Miss Maisie Williams, Montgomeryshire.

KING GEORGE I's CHRISTMAS PUDDING

(This is not to be listed as an economy recipe : nor do Sandringham kitchens prepare it in war-time. But we include it to represent the rich old Christmas tradition.)

KING GEORGE I, sometimes called the " Pudding King," ate this pudding at six o'clock on December 25, 1714—his first Christmas in England. Practically the same ingredients are mixed in huge earthenware bowls at Sandringham for his descendants :

1½ lbs. finely-shredded suet.	1 teaspoonful heaped of mixed
1 lb. eggs, weighed in their shells.	spice.
1 lb. each dried plums, stoned and	½ nutmeg, grated.
halved ; mixed peel, cut in long	2 teaspoonfuls salt.
strips ; small raisins ; sultanas ;	½ pint new milk.
currants ; sifted flour ; sugar	Juice of 1 lemon.
and brown breadcrumbs.	A very large wineglassful brandy.

Mix the dry ingredients, moisten with eggs, beaten to a froth, and the milk, lemon juice and brandy mixed. Stand for at least 12 hours in a cool place, then turn into buttered moulds. Boil for 8 hours at first, then for 2 hours before serving. This quantity makes 3 puddings of about 3 lbs. each.

From Mrs. M. Johnson, Fiskerton, Nottinghamshire.

YULE BREAD

PUT 1 lb. flour into a basin with a pinch of salt. Dissolve ½ oz. yeast in a cupful of warm water and stir into the flour. Let it stand for 1 hour in a warm place then add ½ lb. butter (creamed), ½ lb. sugar, ½ grated nutmeg, ¾ lb. currants, ¼ lb. candied peel and 2 beaten eggs. Mix all together well and pour into tins ; bake in a moderate oven about 2 hours. It is very nice buttered.

From Mrs. L. Butler, Star Farm, Moss, near Doncaster.

CHRISTMAS CAKE WITHOUT EGGS

½ lb. plain flour.
½ lb. ground rice.
½ lb. granulated sugar.
½ lb. currants.
½ lb. sultanas.

¼ lb. mixed peel.
¾ lb. butter or good margarine.
1 teaspoonful bi-carbonate of soda.
12 drops essence of almonds.
½ pint boiling milk.

MIX the flour, rice, sugar, fruit and peel all together. Cream the butter and stir well. Put the soda into a tablespoonful of cold milk, add the essence to the boiling milk, then gradually blend the milk into the mixture while boiling hot. Beat well all together, put into a fairly large tin, and bake in a good oven for 4 hours.

The cake will keep for months and improve.

From Mrs. L. E. Brook, Sussex.

CHRISTMAS CAKE WITH CHERRIES

1 lb. flour.
¼ teaspoonful nutmeg.
¼ teaspoonful cinnamon.
A little salt.
½ lb. butter.
¾ lb. soft sugar (brown).
½ lb. currants.

½ lb. sultanas.
¼ lb. shredded candied peel and almonds.
4 eggs.
Teaspoonful bi-carbonate of soda.
¼ lb. glacé cherries.
½ pint stout or milk.

PASS the flour through a sieve ; add the nutmeg and cinnamon together with the salt. Rub in the butter ; add sugar, currants, sultanas, shredded candied peel and almonds. Lightly beat the eggs, and add the bi-carbonate of soda dissolved in a little milk or water, and mix with the dry ingredients. Add the cherries. Mix with the stout or milk. (The stout gives colour and flavour to the cake.) Put the cake in a well-greased tin ; line the bottom. Bake in a moderate oven.

From Mrs. Hartley, Yorkshire.

MINCE PIES

12 ozs. flour.
9 ozs. butter.

¼ pint cold milk.

RUB lightly into the flour one-third of the butter, add milk, mix into a smooth paste, and roll out into a long narrow strip. Divide remainder of butter into 3 equal portions. Put one portion on paste in small pieces, dredge lightly with flour, fold evenly in three, turn it round so that folded edges lie right and left when rolling. Press edges lightly with rolling pin to prevent air escaping, and roll out as before. Repeat process with other portions of butter. Then roll out to about a ¼ in.

in thickness, and cut covers for pies. Roll pieces out thinner, cut out rounds, and line patty-tins.

Put in some mincemeat, cover with pastry, brush lightly with milk, and dredge with castor sugar. Bake in a hot oven for about 20 minutes. *From Miss A. Griffiths, Montgomeryshire.*

APRICOT MINCEMEAT

1 lb. apricots.	1 lb. brown sugar.
1 lb. dates.	2 ozs. chopped almonds.
1 lb. currants.	½ oz. nutmeg.
1 lb. shredded suet.	The rind and juice of 1 large
1 lb. apples : 1 lb. raisins.	lemon.

SOAK the apricots in a very little cold water overnight. Drain and chop them. Stone the dates and raisins. Peel, core and chop the apples. Add all the other ingredients with grated nutmeg and lemon rind, then add the juice of the lemon.

From Mrs. Scarlett, Bullen Hall, Bramford, Ipswich.

PLUM MINCEMEAT

4 lbs. plums.	4 ozs. peel.
2 lemons.	4 ozs. sweet almonds.
1 teacupful water.	½ oz. ground ginger.
8 large cooking apples.	½ oz. cinnamon and ground
4 ozs. currants.	cloves.
4 ozs. raisins : 4 ozs. sultanas.	1 lb. sugar.

PREPARE the plums, put them in a saucepan with lemon juice and water. Simmer till tender, pass through a sieve. Peel, core and chop the apples. Add the raisins, currants, candied peel and almonds, spices and sugar and the grated lemon rind. Stir well with the plum pulp. Put into jars and seal up.

From Miss Williams, Durham Field Farm, Shotley Bridge, Durham.

MINCEMEAT
(*With Raspberry Jam*)

1 lb. raisins (stoned).	2 lbs. cooking apples (after
1 lb. sultanas.	peeling).
1 lb. currants.	¾ lb. mixed peel.
1 lb. castor sugar.	¾ lb. raspberry jam.
1 lb. suet.	Juice of 3 lemons.
Grated rind of 2 lemons.	1 nutmeg (grated).

MINCE finely the fruit, apples, peel and suet. Stir in sugar, lemon rind and juice, nutmeg and jam. Add a few whole currants and a little brandy or whisky. Mix well, and put into pots and cover closely.

From Miss Margaret Sheffield, Erdington, Birmingham.

WINES AND MEADS

AGRIMONY WINE

A good bunch of agrimony.
2 gallons water.
7 lbs. sugar (Demerara or white).

3 lemons.
6 oranges.
4 ozs. lump ginger.

CRUSH ginger, put with agrimony, and boil in the water until a good colour. Pour liquid on to the sugar, lemons and oranges (sliced), and allow to stand 2 or 3 days. Strain, put into a big jar, and leave to work. The wine, which is exceptionally good for severe colds, can be used after 6 months.

Agrimony can be used freshly gathered or dried. Gather when in full flower. This is in July in the Leicestershire district, where it grows abundantly. Some people may not be acquainted with its name, but no doubt have noticed it in the grass-fields. The plant grows between 1 and 2 ft. in height, and has small yellow flowers growing closely together up the whole of the slender but hard stem.

From Mrs. A. Macer, Leicestershire.

BALM WINE

4 gallons water.
8 lbs. loaf sugar.
Juice of 6 lemons.

Whites of 4 eggs,
1 peck balm leaves.
Slice of toast spread with yeast.

BOIL together the water, sugar, lemons and white of eggs, well beaten, for ¾ hour, skimming well. Then take the balm leaves, put them in a tub with the thin peeling of the lemons; pour the boiling liquor on, stirring well until almost cold. Put on top the toast spread with yeast. Let it work for 2 or 3 days, then strain off, squeezing the leaves through a cloth and afterwards through a flannel bag into a cask. Stop lightly until it has done hissing, then bung down close. At the end of 3 months, bottle. July is the best time for making this tonic drink.

From Mrs. M. E. Moulam, Derbyshire.

BLACKBERRY WINE

PLACE alternate layers of ripe blackberries and sugar in wide-mouthed jars; and allow to stand for 3 weeks. Then strain off the liquid and bottle; adding a couple of raisins to each bottle. Cork lightly at first and later more tightly. Nothing could be more inexpensive and the wine will keep in good condition for a year, having a flavour rather like that of good port.

From Mrs. A. Clayton, Nettleham Well, Misson, Doncaster.

BURNET WINE

TO every quart of Burnet Heads add 2 quarts of boiling water. Let stand 24 hours. Strain, and to every quart of juice add 1 lb. sugar. Boil well for 20 minutes. Pour into a jar and to every 3 quarts of juice add 1 lemon and 1 orange sliced. Let stand until lukewarm. Toast and put on the top a thick slice of bread, spread with 1 oz. yeast. Stand 24 hours, strain again, then stand it in a warm place 6 weeks before bottling. Keep 12 months before using.

From Mrs. T. Coulthard, Silloth, Carlisle, Cumberland.

BLACK CURRANT WINE

4 gallons ripe currants.   6 lbs. loaf sugar.
2½ gallons water.

PUT the currants into a large earthen jar with a cover to it. Boil the water with the sugar, carefully remove the scum as it rises on the liquid, and pour, still boiling, on the currants. Let it stands for 48 hours. Next strain the whole through a flannel bag into another vessel, return it thence into the jar, let it stand a fortnight to settle, then bottle off. Excellent for colds and coughs in winter.

From Mrs. T. J. Mayne, Buckinghamshire.

BROOM WINE

1 gallon water.   Rind and juice of 2 lemons and
3 lbs. lump sugar.   2 oranges.
1 gallon broom flowers.   2 tablespoonfuls yeast.

BOIL sugar and water together with the lemon and orange rinds for ½ hour. When lukewarm pour over the flowers, picked from the stalks, and the juice of lemons and oranges. Stir in the yeast and allow to ferment 3 days. Put into a clean dry cask and allow to work for about a week or ten days, filling up as required. Then stop up close and keep for 6 months or longer when an excellent drink will be found. This is a very old recipe given me by my grandmother, and the wine should be made during May.

From Mrs. N. Fennell, Benton Green, Berkswell, Coventry.

CELERY WINE

THERE is always a waste of the outside pieces of celery: here is a recipe which makes from them an excellent wine, and is also good for those who suffer from rheumatism.

To each pound of green or outside stalks of celery allow 1 quart of water and boil all until tender. Then strain the liquid off and allow 3 lbs. Demerara sugar and ½ oz. of yeast to each gallon put into the cask. Keep the cask well filled up until all the yeast has worked out, and close the bung lightly until the wine is quite still. Then close firmly, leave for a year and bottle off, when it will be ready for use.

From Mrs. Scarlett, Bullen Hall, Bramford, Ipswich.

RED CLOVER WINE

2 quarts of purple blossom.	2 oranges.
4 quarts boiling water.	4 lbs. white sugar.
3 lemons.	1 oz. yeast on toast.

POUR the boiling water over the blossoms. Stand until lukewarm. Slice lemons and oranges, add sugar and the yeast on toast. Put all together in a bowl, stand for 5 days, and stir twice each day. Next strain, and stand for another 5 days. Strain again, leave for 3 days, then bottle, leaving corks loose for 10 days. Then cork up, and it will be ready in a month.

From Mrs. W. Skelton, Cumberland.

CHERRY WINE

I MAKE this from the cracked and windfall Morella cherries that are unsaleable.

After stalking and washing the fruit, place in a crock and add cold water, allowing 1 pint to each pound of fruit. Stir each day for 10 days, then mash well with the hands and leave another 10 days, stirring daily. Then place muslin over another pan. It is a good plan to tie this on. Then, by standing a colander on 2 laths over this, the bulk of the fruit is retained in the colander and enables the liquid to strain through the muslin more easily.

Do not squeeze or hurry it: when all is strained, measure,

and to each quart of liquid add 1 lb. granulated sugar. Stir well and leave till dissolved; then put into big stone bottles, filling to the top. Leave to ferment, filling up as the liquid lowers in the bottles. When quite finished fermentation, cork lightly and let stand at least 6 months before using. It is not so good if used earlier, though a nice drink.

From Miss H. Jenner, Bramble Cottage, Well Street, Loose, Maidstone.

COLTSFOOT WINE

To each gallon of water allow:

2 quarts coltsfoot flowers.	1 lemon.
3 lbs. sugar.	1 orange.
½ lb. raisins.	A little yeast spread on toast.

MEASURE the flowers, put into pan or tub with the right proportion of raisins and rind of the lemon and orange. Put the sugar and water into a saucepan with the lemon and orange juice, bring to the boil, and while boiling pour over the flowers and stir well. Cover and leave till lukewarm. Add a little yeast spread on toast. Leave to ferment for 4 days. Strain into cask, reserving some for filling up. When fermentation subsides, cork down and leave for 6 months.

From Mrs. W. Fennell, Warwickshire.

COWSLIP MEAD

TO every gallon of water allow 2 lbs. of honey: and boil ¾ hour, skimming well. Take 1 pint of the liquor and slice into it 1 large lemon, then pour remainder into an earthenware bowl and put in 1 gallon of cowslip heads. Stir well, cover, and set in a warm place for 24 hours.

Stir in the lemon liquor, 2 sprigs of sweet brier (optional), and ¼ oz. yeast, dissolved in a little of the honey. Let it work for 4 days, then strain into a cask. Keep in a cool place for 6 months, then bottle.

From Mrs. E. Symes, Farnham Tilery, Sharperton, Morpeth, Northumberland.

COWSLIP WINE

4 quarts freshly-picked cowslip flowers, free from stalks and bits of green.	1 lemon.
	1 juicy orange.
	2 tablespoonfuls yeast.
4 quarts boiling water.	A little brandy, if liked.
3 lbs. loaf sugar.	

PARE the rinds very thinly from the orange and lemon, halve the fruit and press out the juice. Put this with the rinds into a tub or pan, and pour on the boiling water in which the sugar has been simmered for ½ hour. (Any scum rising to the top while simmering should be carefully skimmed off.) When the liquid is luke warm, stir in the flowers and yeast, and leave the tub covered with a cloth or flannel for 3 days, stirring twice a day. Then strain the liquid off, and pour it nearly all into a cask, leaving the bung loose till all working has stopped. Fill up with liquor kept over for the purpose, and bung up close. Leave undisturbed for 3 months before using. A little brandy will greatly improve it, but it is not necessary.

From Mrs. A. E. Brooker, Berkshire.

CRAB APPLE WINE

PUT 1 gallon of sliced crab apples into a gallon of water, and let them soak for a fortnight. Strain and add 3 lbs. of Demerara sugar to each gallon of liquor. Stir well and frequently until fermentation takes place, which should be in a day or a day and a half. Leave for 3 days, and then put wine into cask or jar. Lay muslin over the opening until the hissing noise (which tells that the wine is working) has ceased. Then cork tightly, and bottle after 3 months.

This wine is one of the most delicious of our country wines, and improves with keeping.

From Mrs. C. Butchart, Lancashire.

DAMSON WINE

CARE must be taken that the fruit is ripe, sound and unbroken. Wipe and pick over 12 lbs. of damsons, and pour over them 1½ gallons of boiling water. Cover over immediately with a heavy cloth and leave for 4 days, stirring occasionally with a wooden spoon. Strain the fruit from the juice and add to every gallon of the latter 3½ lbs. of loaf sugar ; then pour the wine into a cask, covering the bung-hole with some thick material until fermentation is over, when the bung should be inserted.

In a year the wine may be bottled. I have some of this wine which is 2 years old and is nearly equal to port.

From Mrs. G. Dams, Manor Farm, Glaston, Uppingham.

DANDELION WINE

3 quarts flowers.
1 gallon water.
3 lbs. sugar.

The rind and pulp of 2 lemons and
1 orange.
1 oz. yeast.
1 lb. raisins.

THE flowers must be freshly gathered, picked off their stalks, and put into a large bowl. Bring the water to the boil, pour over the dandelions, and leave for 3 days, stirring each day. Cover the bowl with butter-muslin. After the third day, add the sugar and the rinds only of the lemons and orange. Turn all into a pan and boil for 1 hour. Put back into the bowl and add the pulp of the lemons and orange. Allow to stand till cool, then put in the yeast. Let it remain covered for 3 days, when it will be ready to strain, and put into bottles. The bottles should not be quite filled, and the raisins should be equally divided amongst them. Do not cork tightly till fermentation ceases. This wine, if made in May or June, is good at Christmas.

From Miss L. Kent, Cheshire.

ELDERBERRY WINE

TAKE 7 lbs. berries and 2 gallons of water. To each gallon of liquid add 3 lbs. best loaf sugar, 1 lb. raisins, $\frac{1}{2}$ oz. ground ginger, $\frac{1}{2}$ oz. whole ginger, bruised, 6 cloves, $\frac{1}{2}$ stick cinnamon, 1 lemon.

Strip the berries from the stalks ; pour boiling water over them. Let them stand for 24 hours, then bruise them well and strain through a hair sieve or jelly bag. Measure the liquid, put into an earthenware pan and add sugar and the lemon cut in slices. Boil the cloves, ginger, raisins and cinnamon in a little of the liquid. Strain and add to the rest of the wine.

Allow to stand for a few days, then take off the cap. Strain again and pour into stone jars or casks. Leave open for a few weeks, continually adding more wine until fermentation ceases. Bung tightly and let it remain for 6 months, then bottle.

From Mrs. F. E. Carter, Waterloo, Holsworthy, Devon.

ELDERFLOWER WINE

2 breakfastcupfuls loosely packed
    elderflowers freed from stems.
1 lb. raisins split but not stoned.
Juice of 1 large lemon.

3¼ lb. loaf sugar.
1 white of egg.
1 gallon water.
1 oz. yeast.

DISSOLVE the sugar in the water, stir in the well-beaten white of egg, bring to boil, boil 30 minutes, then skim. Have ready in an earthenware bowl the prepared elderflowers, the raisins and the lemon juice. Pour over the water mixture. Stir thoroughly; and when a little more than milk warm, add the yeast.

Stir once a day for 10 days, then strain and put into a clean dry stone jar, setting the cork in loosely. When the mixture has done working, cork very tightly : and bottle in six months, taking care to strain through flannel and making sure that the bottles and corks are thoroughly sterilized and dry to receive it.

From Mrs. Whitehorn, Surrey.

MILD BROWN ALE

5 oz. hops.
8 gallons water.
2 oz. yeast.

3 lbs. brown sugar, more or less to taste.

BOIL the hops and water together slowly for 40 to 50 minutes, strain over the sugar; add yeast when the liquor is luke-warm, turn into a pan or tub to ferment for 4 days, then cask or bottle for use as wanted. *From Mrs. F. L. Saunders, Childrey, Berks.*

GINGER BEER
(Without the bitter taste which is apparent if all the white pith of the lemons is not removed)

5 quarts boiling water.
1¼ lbs. sugar.
1 oz. whole ginger, bruised.
2 lemons.

¼ oz. cream of tartar.
Good tablespoonful yeast (about 1 oz.).

REMOVE rinds of lemons as thinly as possible. Strip off every particle of white pith. This needs a very sharp knife. Cut lemons into thin slices, removing pips. Put the sliced lemon into an earthenware bowl with sugar, ginger and cream of tartar, and pour on the boiling water. Leave until blood heat, stir in the yeast, and leave, covered with a cloth, in a moderately warm place, for 24 hours. Skim yeast from the top, strain ginger-beer carefully from the sediment. For bottling screw stoppers are best; if corked, tie corks securely. In 2 days the beer will be ready for use. *From Mrs. Margaret Patrick, Surrey.*

GOOSEBERRY WINE

8 lbs. gooseberries.
2 gallons water.

3 lbs. sugar to each gallon of juice.

WASH, top and tail the gooseberries, which should have been picked before they began to change colour. Bruise them well, either with a rolling-pin or wooden vegetable presser.

Put them in a wooden tub or unglazed earthenware crock. Add water, and mix and mash well. Leave covered with a cloth for 2 days. Then strain and measure the liquid. Put this, together with the proper proportion of sugar, into the vessel. Let it stand until the sugar has dissolved, stirring often. Pour into a cask, and leave in a warm place until the fermentation has ceased; this will probably take about 3 weeks. Then drive in the bung securely. Fit a peg into the vent hole, and every day pull it out to allow any gas to escape. When all seems quite still, close up tightly, and leave in a cool place for 8 months. It will then be ready for bottling. *From Mrs. W. Scott, Essex.*

GORSE WINE

½ gallon flowers.
1 gallon water.
2 ozs. root ginger.
1 oz. compressed yeast.

3 lbs. Demerara sugar.
1 orange.
1 lemon.

SIMMER flowers, water and ginger together for 15 minutes, stir in sugar till dissolved. Slice orange and lemon and add to cooling liquid, and when just warm float yeast on a piece of toast on top. Cover with a folded blanket, leave undisturbed for a week, then skim off the head. Strain into a jar, allow to work for another week before corking tightly. A few raisins and a lump of sugar candy keep it lively. Bottle off in November.

From Miss N. Johnson, Ayrshire.

GRAPEFRUIT CHAMPAGNE

CUT up 7 grapefruit in a pan. Pour over 1 gallon of cold water. Let it stand 10 days, then sieve over 4 lbs. of sugar, and leave another 8 days, stirring every day. Strain into another pan, and remove all scum: let it stand a few more days, remove scum as it rises. Bottle off; ready for drinking in 3 weeks. It is also a good tonic and pick-me-up.

From Mrs. S. Allen, The Cottage, Tur Langton, Leicester.

HONEY BEER

4 quarts water.
1 oz. ground ginger.
1 lb. white sugar.
2 ozs. lime juice.

4 ozs. clear honey.
Juice of 3 lemons.
Large teaspoonful fresh yeast on bread.

BOIL 2 quarts of the water with the ginger for ½ hour. Put in a pan with the white sugar, lime juice, honey, lemon juice, and the remaining 2 quarts water (cold). When just at blood heat, add the yeast spread on a piece of bread. Let it remain for 12 hours, then strain through a muslin bag. Allow to settle for an hour or two, and then bottle.

From Mrs. M. Machin, Yorkshire.

MANGOLD WINE

5 lbs. mangolds.
1 gallon water.
3 lbs. lump sugar.

2 lemons.
2 oranges.
½ oz. yeast.

WASH the mangolds but do not peel. Cut into pieces and boil until tender. Strain, and to every gallon of liquid add sugar and rinds of lemons and oranges, boiling for 20 minutes. Allow to cool. Add juice of lemons and oranges. Stir in the yeast mixed with a little castor sugar. Stir all well together, and put into a clean dry jar or cask. Allow to work for about a week, keeping the jar well filled up while working. When finished working, cork down tight and keep for at least 6 months; but the longer it is kept the better.

From Miss N. Fennell, Warwickshire.

NETTLE BEER

2 gallons nettles.
½ oz. root ginger.
4 lbs. malt.
1 oz. yeast.

2 ozs. hops.
4 ozs. sarsaparilla.
2 gallons water.
1½ lbs. castor sugar.

CHOOSE young nettles. Wash and put into a saucepan with water, ginger, malt, hops and sarsaparilla. Bring to the boil and boil for ¼ hour; put sugar into a large pan or earthenware jar; strain nettle mixture on it. Stir until sugar has dissolved. Beat yeast to a cream, and add, leaving until it begins to ferment; then put into bottles. Cork and tie down with string. This may be used at once. *From Mrs. J Blackford, Worcestershire.*

ORANGE WINE

FOR 26 oranges allow 2 gallons boiling water, and to each gallon of liquor allow 2 lbs. sugar. Wipe the oranges and cut in slices, removing the pips. Place in a tub and cover with the boiling water. Cover up and leave for a week, stirring every day with a wooden spoon. Then strain through a fine sieve, allowing the liquid to drip through on its own accord. Measure, and add sugar in proportion. Put in a cask and bung up after a week. This will be ready in 3 months.

From Mrs. R. Walker, Tewkesbury.

PARSLEY WINE

TO every pound of parsley add 1 gallon of boiling water. Let this stand for 24 hours, then strain and boil the liquor for 20 minutes with 1 oz. of lump ginger, the rind of 2 oranges, and 2 lemons. Then pour the liquor on to 4 lbs. of sugar and add the juice of the oranges and lemons. When nearly cool put ½ oz. of yeast on to a slice of toast, and let stand for 4 days. Strain and bottle but do not cork down until the wine has stopped working.

This makes a delicious wine, and is better for keeping.

From Mrs. F. Eyre, Derbyshire.

PARSNIP WINE

TO each gallon of water take 3 lbs. parsnips cut into pieces ½ in. thick, 2 lemons and 1 orange cut small. Boil until the parsnips are soft, strain and pour over 3 lbs. white sugar ; stir till dissolved and bottle while warm, adding to each bottle a small piece of German yeast (about the size of a marble). Keep the bottles full while fermenting ; after fermentation has ceased, cork and wire. This is an excellent imitation of champagne.

From Miss S. Jarrett, Gorphunpfa Cemmaes, Machynlleth, Mont.

PEAR WINE

ALLOW 1 gallon of sliced pears to each gallon of water, and leave to soak for a fortnight, stirring every day. Strain off and add 3 lbs. of sugar to every gallon of liquor. Stir frequently until fermentation takes place, in a day or two. Leave for 3 days : then pour into a cask, lightly covering the opening until fermentation ceases. Bung tightly and bottle in 3 months. Small hard pears are suitable for this.

From Miss E. Rutherford, Tweedmouth.

PLUM PORT

1 gallon water.   4 lbs. damsons.
4 lbs. sugar.

BOIL water and pour over damsons. Leave until next day. Squeeze and stir daily for 5 days, then strain through a jelly bag. Stir in the sugar, and add 1 breakfastcupful of boiling water, and leave to ferment for 8 days. Then skim, and bottle.

From Miss P. Hutchinson, Durham.

POTATO WINE

TAKE ½ gallon of small potatoes, wash them well and cut them in half. Put them into a pan with 1 gallon of fresh cold water with 3 pieces of root ginger, bring to the boil, boil for 10 minutes.

Have another pan ready, into which you have put 3 lbs. of granulated sugar with 2 sliced oranges and 2 sliced lemons. Strain the potato water on to the sugar, etc., and boil again for ½ hour. When cold, bottle, and as soon as the wine has finished working, cork tightly. No yeast is required.

From Mrs. W. H. Charlwood, Rusper, near Horsham, Sussex.

RHUBARB AND BALM WINE

WIPE and cut up 2 lbs. of rhubarb, put it into a large saucepan, with ½ lb. balm leaves (well washed), and 4 quarts cold water. Bring to the boil and boil 30 minutes. Strain and when lukewarm add ½ oz. yeast, ½ oz. citric acid and 1 lb. to 1½ lbs. Demerara sugar, according to taste. Cover, and let it work for 24 hours, then skim and bottle. It is ready for drinking the same day. This makes a most refreshing and health-giving drink.

From Mrs. Vincent, Mount Pleasant, Up-Ottery, Devon.

ROWANBERRY WINE

WHEN the berries are perfectly ripe is the time to make this delicious wine. To each quart of berries add 1 quart boiling water and a small piece of bruised whole ginger. Let them steep for 10 days ; well stir each day, then strain, and to each quart of liquid add 1 lb. of loaf sugar. When dissolved, bottle up. Do not cork tight until fermentation has ceased.

From Mrs. E. Westcott, Burnicombe Farm, Dunsford, near Exeter.

TREACLE ALE

TAKE 5 quarts boiling water, 2 lbs. treacle, 2 ozs. yeast, sugar if required. Melt the treacle with the boiling water in a crock : if not sweet enough add sugar accordingly. When cold, add 2 ozs. yeast (on toast). Cover closely and leave for 3 days. Then bottle and cork tightly, and tie down, as this ale becomes very strong.

This recipe was handed down from my great-grandmother, and it makes a very good drink. In the lean years of part of last century, this ale was used in many Highland homes instead of milk, with porridge (served in separate bowls) : and a very excellent substitute they considered it.

From Mrs. J. Neil, Drumbauchly, Perth, N.B.

FOR Your CORNER CUPBOARD

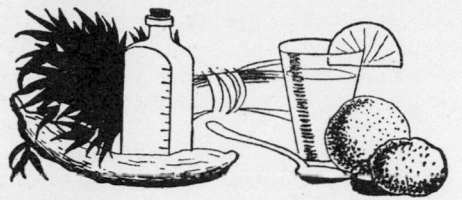

TONIC DRINKS

WINTER CORDIAL

4 dessertspoonfuls fine oatmeal.	1 lemon.
½ teaspoonful ground ginger.	1 quart boiling water.
2 dessertspoonfuls Demerara sugar.	

MIX oatmeal, sugar and ground ginger together in a basin. Grate the rind of the lemon and add. Gradually pour in the boiling water, stirring the while. Put in saucepan, add lemon juice and simmer for 10 minutes. Strain and serve hot.

From Mrs. Westwood, Stratford-on-Avon.

TREACLE POSSET

1 pint milk.	The juice of 1 lemon.
2 tablespoonfuls treacle.	

PUT milk into a saucepan and bring almost to boiling point. Add the treacle and lemon juice and boil slowly until the curd separates. Strain, and serve hot as a remedy for a cold.

From Miss E. Tudor, Cheshire.

NETTLE SYRUP

GATHER the tops of young nettles, wash well; and to every 1 lb. of nettles add 1 quart of water. Put into a pot and boil for 1 hour. Then strain, and to every pint of juice add 1 lb. sugar: boil for 30 minutes, and when cold bottle it up.

This syrup we make from a very old recipe and it is said to have great health-giving powers as a blood purifier. Used with soda water it is a cooling drink.

From Mrs. E. Rutherford, Tweedmouth.

BOTTLED TOMATO JUICE

WIPE and stem ripe tomatoes : cut them in halves and put them, cut side down, in a saucepan, standing it at the back of a warm stove until the juice begins to flow. Press down frequently with a wooden spoon and boil them for 30 minutes. Strain through a fine colander—a soup strainer is ideal—pressing all the juice and most of the pulp through, leaving only skin and pips.

Put the juice back on the stove, add salt, sugar and pepper to taste, boil for 15 minutes. Pour into *hot* sterilized jars or bottles and seal at once. Don't season the juice too highly, as more can be added when served. This makes a most healthful and refreshing drink. It will keep good for 12 months.

From Mrs. D. Esmé Booker, near Leighton Buzzard, Beds.

AN ANCIENT BARLEY DRINK

(Suitable for invalids ; a very effective and nourishing drink for feverish ailments)

2 ozs. pearl barley.	2 ozs. stoned raisins.
5 pints boiling water.	2 ozs. sliced figs.
	½ oz. liquorice root.

WASH and blanch the pearl barley. Add 4 pints of the water and cook until reduced one half. Strain, and to the barley water add the raisins, figs and the other pint of water. Simmer again until reduced to 2 pints, adding the liquorice root just before cooking is completed, then strain.

This compound concoction is to be used, diluted, for drinks, and is suitable for mixing with plain barley water. It can also be given in small quantities without dilution.

From Mrs. E. Farrington, Worcestershire.

LEMON GINGER SYRUP

BRUISE 4 ozs. of whole ginger and put in a saucepan with a quart of water and the thinly-peeled rind of a lemon. Bring to the boil, and boil slowly for about ¾ hour. Strain, measure and to every pint of liquid allow 1 lb. of sugar and the juice of a small lemon. Put the liquid, sugar and lemon into a saucepan, and boil for 10 minutes, skimming well.

When cold, put into bottles and seal. When required put a tablespoonful of the syrup into a tumbler and fill up with boiling water. Put a thin slice of lemon on top and serve at once.

From Mrs. F. Haynes, Bosworth Lodge, Husband's Bosworth, Rugby.

ELDER SYRUP

ELDERBERRIES have tonic and health-giving qualities: this syrup makes the most of them:

Take ½ a gallon of elderberry juice and put it into a brass pan over a clear but slow fire, adding to it the white of an egg well beaten to a froth.

When it begins to boil, skim it as long as any froth rises; then put to each pint 1 lb. of cane sugar, and boil the whole slowly till it is a perfect syrup; which may be known by dropping a particle on your nail, and if it congeals, it is done enough.

Let it stand; and when cool, put into bottles covered with paper pricked full of holes. It will make elderberry wine in winter, and if taken hot is excellent for colds.

From Mrs. V. Bainbridge, Frensham, Surrey.

BLACKBERRY CORDIAL

POUR 1 pint of white wine vinegar over 1 quart of ripe blackberries. Let it stand in an earthenware jar for 7 or 8 days, stirring meanwhile to extract the juices. Strain off when ready, and put the liquor in an enamel saucepan with 1 lb. of loaf sugar and ½ lb. of honey. Bring to the boil, then remove from the heat and allow it to get cold. Bottle and cork and keep it in a dark place. This is an excellent winter remedy for colds and sore throats, a tablespoonful in a glass of hot water making a pleasant bedtime drink.

From Mrs. A. D. Underwood, Margaret Roding, near Dunmow, Essex.

TONIC STOUT

8 ozs. black (or burnt) malt.	2 medium-sized potatoes.
1 oz. hops.	2 oz. brown sugar.
1 oz. dried stinging nettles.	1 oz. yeast.
¼ oz. black liquorice.	10 pints water.

WHEN the water is at boiling point add herbs, malt, hops, liquorice, and the potatoes (well washed but not peeled, and perforated by a fork or darning needle). Simmer gently for 1 hour, then strain into a pan, earthenware, if possible. Add sugar. When about 95° F. stir in the yeast, which has been dissolved in a little of the warm liquid. Cover up, and stand for 24 hours. Skim off yeast, and put in jar or bottles; corking lightly at first, tightening up 12 hours later. Leave for 2 days. You will then find it a beautiful creamy stout, with remarkable tonic properties.

From Miss A. Foster, Hampshire

SALVES AND COUNTRY CURES
ELDERFLOWER OINTMENT

1 lb. pure vaseline.   Elderflowers.

PUT the vaseline into a saucepan with as many elderflowers (not the thick stems) as can possibly be pressed into it. Allow to simmer (*not boil*) for ½ to ¾ hour. While very hot, strain through a piece of muslin into small pots.

It is ready for use as soon as it is cold.

This is good for heat lumps, bites, chapped or rough hands, and excellent for a baby in case of rash or roughness of the skin. It is equally suitable for young and old.

From Mrs. F. W. Lawley, The Lodge, Fitzjohns Farm, Great Canfield,
Essex.

ANOTHER ELDERFLOWER OINTMENT

1 lb. lard (clarified).   1 gallon elderflower heads.

MELT the lard, put in the elderflowers and boil till pulped. Strain through a gravy strainer, and put in a few drops of turpentine. Pour into small jars, and leave to set. My mother and grandmother made this salve every year, and fifty years of testing have increased its reputation.

From Mrs. H. Guest, Whisketts Farm, Lamberhurst, Kent.

OLD-FASHIONED SULPHUR SALVE

MIX equal portions of home-made lard and flowers of sulphur to a smooth paste. This very simple ointment is ready for use immediately, and has always been a wonderfully quick cure for most affections of the skin.

From Mrs. Wynne, Pidham Farm, Langrish, Petersfield, Hants.

FARMHOUSE HERB SALVE

This salve is excellent for all sores and bruises ; and is particularly good also as a veterinary aid for softening the udders of newly-calved cows, or for sore teats. Its healing properties are remarkable.

1 lb. home-rendered lard.   1 good handful of each of the
                                    following : elderflowers,
                                    wormwood, groundsel.

CUT the herbs into 1-in. lengths. Put into an earthenware pot with the lard, and bring to the boil in the oven. Simmer for ½ hour. Then strain into pots and tie down when cool. This salve can be made from dried herbs, but it is better to use them fresh.   *From Mrs. Catherine Mary Drury, Pinxton, Notts.*

DRESSING FOR A SPRAIN

TAKE equal parts of glycerine and castor oil; and add to them a little beeswax which you have melted in readiness. Mix well together. This is a simple and soothing unguent.

From Miss M. E. Rivers, Frensham, Surrey.

A GOOD LINIMENT

1 cupful vinegar.   A piece of camphor.
1 cupful turpentine.   1 egg.

A GOOD old-fashioned liniment for sprains and chilblains can be made from the above ingredients. Mix all together well in a bottle until the resulting liquid is white and creamy. It is then ready for use.

From Miss E. Woodmansey, Yorkshire.

GRANDMOTHER'S EMBROCATION

TAKE ½ pint of turpentine and 1 egg: put them together into a large bottle. Cork it and shake it till it becomes a cream; then add gradually 1 pint of vinegar and a small tablespoonful of liquid ammonia, and bottle for use. This embrocation keeps for years in well-corked bottles.

From Mrs. A. D. Jones, Stoep House, Hooton Park, Cheshire.

MEDICINAL JAM

1 lb. prunes.   1 lb. Demerara sugar.
1 lb. seedless raisins.   ¼ lb. whole almonds.

REMOVE the stones from the prunes. Chop prunes and raisins very finely, together with the blanched almonds and the kernels from the prune stones. Soak all overnight in 1 pint of water. Next day add the Demerara sugar, bring to the boil, and cook for ½ hour; boiling not too fast. Pour into hot jars and seal down immediately. If you can spare the sugar to make this jam, you will find that it is delicious (especially on brown bread); and is a mild natural laxative for children.

From Mrs. M. Johnstone, Benwell, Northumberland.

CUCUMBER LOTION
(*For weather-roughened skins*)

CUT 6 ripe cucumbers into slices about ½ in. thick. Steam till soft enough to pass through a colander, then press again through a piece of butter muslin. Measure the pulp;

and for every 3 ozs. allow $\frac{1}{2}$ pint of distilled rose water, $\frac{1}{2}$ drachm of powdered borax, and 25 drops of simple tincture of benzoin. Dissolve the borax in the rose water, add the benzoin drop by drop, shaking the bottle frequently. Lastly, add the rose water to the pulp and shake again thoroughly. Apply night and morning after washing the face and neck.

From Mrs. C. Bartram, Harefield, Cecil Park, Pinner.

HONEY COUGH MIXTURE

PUT into a bottle 4 ozs. pure cod liver oil, 1 oz. of glycerine, 4 ozs. of honey (pure), and the strained juice of 3 lemons. Shake well.

This mixture should be taken 3 times a day after meals, and shaken well always before pouring.

From Mrs. Kingston, Richhill, Co. Armagh.

THE HOUSEHOLD SHELF
FURNITURE CREAM (1)

MELT 3 ozs. white wax, pour on 8 ozs. turpentine, add 8 ozs. warm water. Drop in sufficient liquid ammonia to thicken to a cream. This was my great-grandmother's recipe : the only difference being that I have replaced yellow wax, which she used, by the white wax, which I find better.

From Mrs. A. Leath, Hall Farm, Mantby, Yarmouth.

FURNITURE CREAM (2)

$\frac{1}{2}$ pint turpentine.	1 oz. white wax.
$\frac{1}{2}$ pint soft water.	2 squares camphor.
2 ozs. beeswax.	1 oz. Castile soap.

SHRED fine the waxes and camphor into the turpentine. Shred soap, put into the water and simmer until the quantity is reduced to half. Then let cool a little. Now mix all together and add 1 spoonful of ammonia ; be careful when adding this. Shake well. You will find your trouble well rewarded.

From Mrs. A. Wilson, White Rock House, Bradwell, Sheffield.

FURNITURE REVIVER

TAKE equal parts of turpentine, linseed oil and vinegar, Add 1 teaspoonful of granulated sugar to each $\frac{1}{2}$ pint of polish, and shake well. This is a cleanser as well as a polish.

From Mrs. Gladys Kimble, Valley Farm, Soulbury, Leighton Buzzard.

THREE-IN-ONE CLEANER

SHRED into a pan ¼ lb. white Castile soap, and pour on 2 quarts boiling water. Simmer until soap dissolves. Add ½ oz. saltpetre. Stir well: strain. Now add (carefully) ½ pint ammonia. Bottle and cork tightly.

Damp your *carpets*, brush in some of the cleanser, and clean off with a sponge and clean water. Add enough whitening to make a thin cream, and you have a wonderful cleanser for *white paint*. Make the cream a bit thicker, and it cleans *silver*.

From Miss M. Scarlett, Bullen Hall, Ipswich.

SCOURING POWDER

SHAKE up 1 lb. whitening, 1 lb. pumice powder and 1 lb. soap powder to make a good cleanser economical to prepare and to use. *From Mrs. A. Hartley, Moneymore, Co. Derry.*

POLISHING CLOTHS

DISSOLVE ½ lb. of shredded soap in ½ pint of boiling water, and then add 4 ozs. of whitening and a tablespoonful cf ammonia. Beat this till it is a smooth jelly ; then lay in it some squares of soft linen and let them soak for 12 hours. Next day squeeze them out, and leave to dry. These cloths are really magic polishers, and are excellent for silver and all metals.

From Miss Joyce Francis, Alconbury House Farm, Huntingdon.

" REVIVER " FOR BLUE FABRICS

This preparation is for the cleaning and reviving of navy or dark blue woollen materials, suits, greatcoats, uniforms, blazers, gym tunics, felt hats, etc.

TAKE a saucepan, an old one for preference—iron or enamel, not brass or copper—and fill it full of ordinary green ivy leaves. When as many as possible have been pressed into the pan, cover with cold water and bring to the boil. After boiling for 20 minutes, stand the pan by the side of the stove and simmer for 3 hours. Strain off the leaves and to every pint of liquid, add 1 tablespoonful of liquid ammonia. Put into a bottle and cork, and for safety label " Poison." It keeps indefinitely.

Spread the garment to be cleaned on a table, and, with a cloth (preferably a piece of old blue serge), sponge, giving extra attention to the most soiled patches. Press with an iron afterwards.

From Mrs. Kate Carding, Carr Banks, Farnsfield, near Newark, Notts.

INDEX

Index

Index

Printed in Great Britain by The Campfield Press, St. Albans